DISCOVER THE POWER WITHIN YOU

Arun H. Raikar

Published by
Ocean Books (P) Ltd.
4/19 Asaf Ali Road,
New Delhi-110 002 (INDIA)
e-mail: info@oceanbooks.in

ISBN 978-81-8430-554-8
DISCOVER THE POWER WITHIN YOU

Edition
2025

Price
₹ 300.00 (Rupees Three Hundred only)

Printed at
Royal Offset, Delhi

DISCOVER THE POWER WITHIN YOU

Other Important Books on Self Help

Title	Author	Price
• A to Z of Success	Y.S. Rajan	300.00
• Mantras of Success	Sanjay Chadha	200.00
• Take it or Leave it	S.N Roy	125.00
• Managing Marriage	HS Srivastava	225.00
• Managing Sadness	Arun K. Tiwari	250.00
• Broken Brains	Arun K. Tiwari	250.00
• Inner View : Psychology of Dreams	Arun K. Tiwari	200.00
• Doctor Story of Life & Death	Subbarao/Tiwari	300.00
• The Art of Positive Thinking	Arvind Narayan	200.00
• Let us Learn Meditation	Arvind Narayan	200.00
• Let us Learn Numerology	Anita Bhatnagar	150.00
• Let us Learn Astrology	Rakesh Bhasin	150.00

Preface

We all want success in our life. Success means big money, higher responsibility, respect and greater satisfaction. We hate failures. No matter who we are. No matter what we do. Failures are simply not acceptable to us.

But there still are people who accept failures as their fate. They are discontent, but don't dream success, as they have convinced themselves that they don't have the quality necessary for bigger accomplishments.

There is a misconception about success. There are those who assume that success is reserved only for a particular class, and that it is something beyond their reach. They also presume that they don't have the qualities or the assets necessary for major accomplishments.

This is why most people throughout their life are steeped in mediocrity. They accept whatever fate brings them. There are only a few who reach the top. Not because they have extraordinary intellect. Not because they have extraordinary qualifications. In fact, you will find that many of them are just as average as any other person. If you sincerely delve a little further, you will find that on many assets you will outrank them.

Then which is the force that helps them move up the ladder?

We all have tremendous reservoirs of qualities and huge stocks of powers hidden inside us. The only thing required is to discover them. You will agree that each one of us is a very good combination of pluses and minuses. No one is perfect, no one is custom-made. Sometimes we face failures because we tend to overlook where things went wrong. Sometimes we find that the goal set by us is not clear. That's because the lens through which we look at the goal itself is not clear.

Those, whom you consider successful have discovered their powers and polished them. That is what this book will do for you.

Most of the stories narrated in the book are true stories. Some are based on the facts of life. I have intentionally changed the names or used only symbolic identifications to protect the actual identities. The examples quoted show only masculine gender. This has been done only for ease in writing, but the principles are equally applicable for both the genders.

While going through the chapters, you will easily recognise the characters around you. You will find that you come across these characters day in and day out.

—Arun H. Raikar

Phone. (0731)2321271
Mobile: 9926573744
E-mail: a_h_raikar@yahoo.com

How to Read this Book

This book is based on certain principles and facts of life. To understand them better it is advisable to read the book slowly and carefully, one chapter at a time. The whole book cannot be absorbed in a single stroke reading. Move on to the next chapter only after making sure you have understood the previous chapter fully.

If possible read the book with a group. May be your spouse, your children, your colleagues or your friends, with whom you may like to exchange your views. Discuss with them about your opinion on the subject matter. By doing so, you will find that many big and useful ideas emerge. Also, you will find that the book has a greater concern with the real facts of your life.

This book is in your hands. It proves that you believe in progress, and are determined to achieve greater success in life. I hope the book will provide the necessary tools, and will help you move up the ladder into the 'uncrowded world of success'. Good luck.

Gratitude

Any accomplishment is a result of collective wisdom and collective endeavour, and this book is no exception. When I thought of using the experience that I had during the last 25 years of my professional career and give it the shape of a book, it seemed somewhat difficult, as the episodes were scattered and it was an ambitious task to arrange them in order. Further it was a greater task to use them properly so that they portray the message of each chapter correctly.

I am grateful to my friends who helped me a lot and especially to my wife 'Sunanda' and my son 'Koustubh' for their valuable suggestions from time to time. Without their patience and support it would not have been possible to give my thoughts the shape of this book. I thank my friend 'Ismail Lahri' who made several cartoons exclusively for my book, which illustrate the theme of the chapters effectively.

Most of the stories in this book are true life stories experienced by me, some of the examples however are the outcome of a collection from various sources like newspapers, magazines and seminars or lectures that I have attended over the last 25 years. But it was impossible to memorise the correct sources of them, as they were not noted down. I, however, express my sense of gratitude to all of them for their contribution to this book, regardless of their individual identity.

Contents

1. No Flowers Blossom under the Shadow 13
2. A Sincere Effort is Always Helped 21
3. Eradicate Fear 25
4. Recognise Your Strengths 34
5. Keep Your Attitude Positive 49
6. Ensure Your Environment is Clean 62
7. Small Habits that Matter 68
8. Importance of Timely Action 73
9. Identify Your Goal 80
10. Don't Overlook Great Ideas 88
11. Communicate Effectively 94
12. Think Creatively 103
13. Be an Effective Leader 107
14. Use the Manpower Smartly 131
15. Remember 139

There is a winner hidden deep down within you. Discover your winner and be an achiever.

No Flowers Blossom under the Shadow

A good friend of mine loved horticulture and gardening. He always cherished love for lush green surroundings, which he never got till he was in metros, as the small flats of metros had no scope for gardening.

When he got transferred over to our small town, he opted for a huge house, which had enough scope for gardening. He was very happy, as his long cherished dream for lush green surroundings would come true now. He, without losing any time brought varieties of plants and of course the seeds of carpet lawns.

He took pains to nurse the plants. He woke-up early mornings and spent hours to water them. Soon the lawns grew thick and many plants were laden with colourful flowers.

But what disappointed my friend was that a corner of the garden did not grow lawns, neither the plants in this corner grew beautiful flowers. No fertilisers or pesticides worked in this corner. No plants flourished in this particular corner.

No flowers blossom under the shadow

It was observed that while the entire area was exposed to the open weather, this particular corner remained under the shadow of a huge tree. The shadow of this large tree made a big circle on the ground covering a quarter of the garden. Many boosters were tried but all in vain.

Often the branches of the tree entangled in the electricity wires causing thereby interruption in the power supply. Further it also invited risk to human lives in the rainy season.

Finally it was decided to cut the tree. It was cut-down leaving only the stem behind. And suddenly we found that the small plants started growing. Flowers began blossoming on these plants. The dry corner of the garden grew thick spongy lawns.

Actually this is a natural phenomenon of life, and is equally applicable to all of us. Some people start behaving like a scapegoat when they are exposed to challenges. They display such behaviour, as they have never developed the habit of working independently. They feel helpless, deprived and handicapped when the shelter is removed. It should be noted here that the purpose of writing this is not to criticise the shelter. In fact each one of us needs shelter in some or the other way. Children need shelter of the parents during their childhood to grow strong.

But its negative side can be seen when the sense of feeling insecure develops as a 'syndrome'. We may call it the ***shelter syndrome.*** The real problem begins when it does not allow you to grow even when you need to grow independent. Sometimes you need to take important decisions independently and you find yourself in a fix.

When a salesman works in the marketplace, he is expected to take 'spot decisions' in order to save his business interest. He cannot go to his boss every time to ask what he should do and what he shouldn't. He can do it effectively only if he has developed the confidence. Who can tell a high school student better than himself, which subject he should choose?

Remember: "One needs exposure to challenges to develop his own capability."

In fact sometimes we are so used to work in the same moulds that we never try to come out of them. The thought of exposure to challenges terrifies us. **"We take challenges as threats". We do not take challenges as opportunities.** Opportunities come to all of us. Sometimes they come to us in disguise and we fail to recognise them. We take them like we take threats, and deal with them, the way we deal with threats.

Sometimes we behave like a 'domesticated parrot' that does not dare to fly even when the door of the cage is opened. The bird has an open sky in front of him, where nothing hampers his flight and where heights have no limitations. But years of captivation weaken not only his wings, but also clip his desire and 'will power' to fly.

Have you ever heard of a swimmer who learnt

swimming in a bathtub? If you have to learn swimming, you must throw yourself on the ripples of water.

This shelter syndrome hampers the growth of both. If you are protected, the fear of exposure doesn't allow you to grow stronger. If you are a protector, you are still a loser, because your shelter doesn't allow your dependent to fetch you results and you are affected. Remember...opportunities come to all of us. Sometimes they come to us in disguise. It is important to recognise them. The same opportunity will never come to you the next time. It may come with a new face. It may be better; it may be worse, but never the same again.

Mr. Fransis was working as a 'Sales Manager' in a medium sized company dealing in water meters. He had six people reporting to him. Four of them were average and were always waiting for their senior's instructions to act upon. The remaining two were somewhat promising. Let us call them Mr. A. and Mr. B.

When Mr. Fransis's father was on deathbed, he had to proceed on long leave. The management faced a dilemma of who would take charge from Mr. Fransis now to run the show in his absence.

Naturally the two names that came to mind were Mr. A. and Mr. B. As Mr. A. measured higher on the scale of sale-figures, he was called by the director to his office. After some formal discussions the director told Mr. A. that since Mr. Fransis was proceeding on leave, the management expected Mr. A. to run the show till Mr. Fransis was back.

Now actually Mr. A. should have been thankful to the management for the confidence shown by the management in him. Also he should have seen a golden opportunity to prove his mettle, which he undoubtedly had. Further, this opportunity could have paved the way for his growth in future.

But on the contrary Mr. A. saw the threat in the challenge, and not the opportunity. The first thing, which came to his mind was, what would happen if he took a wrong decision? He did not see a bright future hidden. He instead saw a threat to his job.

It was natural that Mr. A. was lost and his face was hung when he came out of the Director's cabin. The best way he chose to avoid any wrong decisions was not to take any decisions even when required. The result was obvious. Pending claims and other important matters started taking the shape of a 'heap'. Collections declined rapidly. Within a week the smooth functioning began to falter.

The management had no options but to call Mr. B. and ask him to take charge.

Mr. B.'s approach was totally different. First of all he thanked the management for showing faith in him and giving him an opportunity. He immediately threw himself into the new assignment. He first reviewed the whole affair and took corrective steps wherever required.

Without disturbing the norms he saw how he could implement his new constructive ideas. He also held a meeting of all colleagues and took them into confidence by telling them that since Mr. Fransis was not there, "our responsibility has increased and that this is the real testing time. We must rise to the occasion." He immediately took steps to ensure that collections came in time. This also increased the sales. Soon the department again resumed its smooth functioning.

It was very natural that when the post of 'Sales Manager' was vacant a few months later, Mr. B. was elevated. Mr. A. had missed the train because of his **'shelter syndrome'.**

Next time when you face a similar situation, ask yourself these questions:

- ❖ Do I take challenges as opportunities or I take them as threats?
- ❖ Does exposure threaten me?
- ❖ Do I fear taking decisions independently?

Remember:

- ❖ Small plants seldom grow under the shadow of a huge tree.
- ❖ Talent does not sparkle under the shelter, like the flowers do not blossom under the shadow.
- ❖ Opportunities come to all of us. Sometimes they come to us in disguise. Don't fail to recognise them.
- ❖ The same opportunity may not come to you again.
- ❖ Exposure to challenges is to help you grow strong.
- ❖ Start taking decisions without fear.
- ❖ Come out of the shelter to grow big and strong.

□

Achievement comes before effort
Only in the dictionary.

A Sincere Effort is Always Helped

All of us have gone to a Railway Station platform. Sometimes to catch the train or sometimes to receive or to see off our loved ones. But we hardly try to take notice of a scene, which is very common.

As the train starts to move, you almost always find a person crossing the over bridge hurriedly. He tries to push the crowd away to clear his way in haste. Have you ever tried to notice what your first reaction is when he rushes on to you? You hurriedly move apart to clear his way. You don't have to try to act this way. Your action is spontaneous.

Have you ever tried to think why you act this way?

You act this way, because in your conscious or subconscious mind you know that he is sincerely trying to catch the train. Now what is your next reaction? You pull out a leg and stretch your neck out to watch eagerly whether he catches the train or not. As soon as you find that he has, with great efforts managed to board the train, you heave a sigh of relief. Again this action is spontaneous. You do not have to try to act this way. Somewhere in your 'conscious' or 'subconscious' mind you are supportive to him. That is why you feel relaxed, as you find that he has boarded the train.

Why do you heave a sigh of relief when you find that he has finally got into the train? Naturally because (again) the effort was sincere.

Now, what is the reaction of those, already on the train? One of the passengers standing by the door extends a helping hand and pulls him up. He also takes care that the new fellow passenger does not fall while boarding the train.

Neither have the two met before, nor would they meet again. Then what inspires the passenger to extend a helping hand to a person not known to him?

My dear friends...the answer again is, a 'sincere effort' and 'only sincere effort'.

Now imagine for a while, how you would react if you found that the passenger was walking in a casual manner towards the train. Would you still help him? Obviously you won't. Possibly you would not even bother to look at him. Neither would the passengers already on the train extend a helping hand. Because they know that the new fellow is not sincerely trying, and that he is not bothered even if he doesn't get the train.

Remember, this is a natural phenomenon in our life. Often we tend to think that an honest and real help is only a speculation. But you will always find that there are people ready to extend a helping hand. The only condition is that your effort has to be sincere.

Always remember:

People help and respect a person who puts in an honest effort.

In our office the peon was always busy running in and out, as he always had to go to a neighbouring Xerox copy centre. The work would come in lots, one after the other. Looking at the workload, the urgency to have our own xerox-copier was keenly felt.

When we inquired about the prices and features, several quotations poured in with literature. One of these quotations came to us through a salesman, who not only submitted the offer, but also took extra pains to explain the features of his copier to us. He frequently visited our office to know the fate of our requirement.

The price range of all the copiers was nearly the same, so it didn't really matter much, which machine we would choose. As about the quality, all the machines had some pluses and some minuses.

Now, the only factor, which had a direct effect on our decision, was a personal follow-up. It was obvious that we chose the copier, which had a strong support of frequent visits by the salesman. He could get the business only because of his honest effort.

Remember, if your effort is honest and sincere, you get help not only from your friends, but also from those who are in no way related to you, or may be they don't even know you.

Basically a human being is not unsupportive unless

he or she is damaged by somebody's success. Sometimes a typical 'unsupportive' behaviour is seen, but those who have negative thinking, display such behaviour. And you naturally cannot expect such people to help you.

Next time when you face a situation, where you earnestly need somebody's help, remember that:

People help and respect a person who puts in an honest effort.

□

Eradicate Fear

This is important, as fear is the biggest enemy in one's success. Fear stops people from capitalising on an opportunity. Fear stops you from speaking, when you want to speak. Fear creates worry, frustration and develops a feeling of being unimportant and inferior. The result is, you keep watching beside the road, while others drive away.

We often see that before an examination or an important interview, when a person is hit by fear, his friends try to encourage him just by saying—"Don't worry", every thing will be all right. While saying this they really mean that there is nothing to be afraid of, but is it really possible to eliminate fear merely by saying that everything will be all right? We all know that this kind of medicine really doesn't work. Fear is a state of mind and nothing more than that. But it is real and it is the biggest enemy in one's success.

When there is some disorder in your body, you go to a physician who conducts some tests to find out the cause of the disorder. When he discovers, he doesn't stop there. He proceeds with treatment. Simply telling you the name of the disease doesn't cure it.

Similarly fear can be cured only by action. Do you remember how you learnt driving a motorbike or a car?

It was so difficult. The thought of other vehicles on the road terrified us. Young boys driving their bikes harshly and heavy vehicles running on the road came first to our mind.

What did you do then? Did you give up the idea of learning how to drive your vehicle? Obviously not. Once you drove the vehicle for a few minutes, you found that you had destroyed the fear. In other words, we can say that fear was cured only by action.

Yes—fear can be eradicated only by action. It is true that fear is only a state of mind. But it is so big and so effective a negative force that it always drags you behind, and you find that others have gone a long way ahead leaving you trailing behind.

A few years ago, in a very useful training session on 'effective presentation skills' each participant was asked, what the main problem was that he faced while making a presentation. Most of the participants had some or the other problem. But it was quite amazing to see that everyone's problem had a relation with the audience, the problem relating to the persons sitting on the other side.

A very senior member of the team said, "the thought that those sitting in the audience may have a better knowledge of the subject", had a great effect on his presentation.

This is true. When on the dais for the first time, it is

quite likely that you will develop a feeling that the persons sitting in front of you, down there in the audience may be more knowledgeable, and that what would happen if they know more of the subject, on which you have to make your presentation.

Why do the other people look frightfully big, frightfully important?

In the first place be clear that the other fellow is still a human being, just another human being like you, having the same interests, desires and problems like you. If you are there on the dais to speak, he is down there in the audience to listen to you. Even if he knows many things on the subject, he is still there to listen to you, because there can be at least one point, which he can know and learn from you.

Negative and unpleasant thoughts deposited in the mind affect your skills. They create needless fear and worry, and develop a feeling of being inferior. **The result is, once you falter while speaking, others stare at you. Their sharp stare shakes your confidence, and you start acting like a drowning man having a crowd of spectators just standing there waiting for you to sink away.**

To avoid such unpleasant situation there are a few remedies that will help you eradicate fear.

Don't be a backbencher

You must have noticed in a business meeting, classroom sessions, conferences or other assemblies, the back seats fill up first. People sometimes literally scramble to sit in the back rows. Such behaviour is to make sure that they are not too conspicuous. Hiding yourself behind the front seats to avoid being conspicuous, shows nothing but lack of confidence.

Next time when you try to occupy a back seat, ask yourself—"what am I trying to hide?", "from whom am I trying to hide?", and most importantly, "why am I trying to hide?"

Practise sitting in the front row. It will build up confidence. So what if you are visible. Always occupy the front seat, as taking shelter behind the front seats or hiding yourself behind them is like playing hide and seek with success.

Let your eyes work for you

Eyes are the best and the easiest way to judge a person. How a person uses his eyes, tells us a lot about him. A person avoiding to make eye contact gives us a wrong message about him. By avoiding making eye contact, he tells you that—I feel weak before you, or I am afraid of you, or I feel inferior, or I feel guilty and I have done something wrong which I don't want you to know. If you are clear in your conscience, there is no need to avoid making eye contact. Avoiding making eye contact says nothing good about you.

Looking directly in the other person's eyes tells him that—I'm honest, you can trust me, I'm not afraid of you and I'm confident.

Make your eyes work for you. Aim them directly at

the other person's eyes. It will not only give you confidence, but it will also win you confidence.

Practise speaking up

After every business meeting or a conference, I have found that many people exchange their views with others. Sometimes the views are really impressive, but of no use, as they remained calm in the forum. The reason was only lack of confidence.

Why does a person prefer to keep quiet even when he wants to participate? It is because he thinks that his opinion is probably worthless. "If I say something, I'll probably look foolish. By saying something, people will know how ignorant I am, and that other people might know more than I do." The fellow thinks to himself that he will speak the next time. Each time he fails to speak, he feels more inadequate and more inferior. He makes a promise to himself to speak the next time, although he knows he will not. With every time failing to speak he becomes smaller. With every failure he feels more inferior.

If you have the same problem, if you are shy of speaking, make sure, you actively participate in every meeting. **If you don't speak up today, next time it will be more difficult, as every single failure will reduce your confidence level and make you smaller.**

In contrast, if you speak up today, next time it will be easier for you to speak. **"Waiting for suitable or perfect conditions to speak, means waiting for ever".** If you speak today, you will definitely find it easier the next time and every time. Also you will use your energy and knowledge not for gathering courage to speak, but to think something creative.

Don't wait for the perfect conditions to speak, as they will never be. And don't worry. You won't look foolish if you speak. You will find it easier the next time if you speak today. Participate in every business meeting. Ask questions. Make suggestions. Give your opinion. This will eradicate fear.

How postures are important: Do your postures play any role in life? How important is your body language? Does it affect your mental interior?

Yes. It does. Your body language tells a lot about you. Not only this, it also affects your thinking process. Correct postures give you strength and project a positive image about you. Clumsy postures or defensive body language reduce your size.

Have you ever noticed how some people feel uncomfortable when they are on the dais? Especially when they are under focus for the first time? When called on the dais, most people try to hide their fear (and look normal), but fail to do so only because of wrong postures. Many people put their hands in the pockets of trousers. This is a defensive posture and doesn't speak anything good about them. This type of posture creates an impression that the person is afraid of those present there. Some people lock their arms with each other or clasp the palms keeping them in front of the zip. All these postures produce a defensive image. They create the image of a person afraid of exposure. These types of postures destroy one's confidence.

The correct posture is the one, which projects you as a confident person. Instead of hiding your hands in your pockets, or locking your arms in front of the zip, keep one palm on the other at the height of your waist. This posture speaks of a confident person. There is no need to hide your hands. It will be better (and you will find it easier too) if you carry a piece of paper or a diary in your hand. This will help you maintain the correct posture. More importantly, make sure you don't fumble with the things like the buckle of your belt or neck-tie.

You will find that most people, who are not taken seriously, are treated like that not because of others, but because of themselves. Know it well that people see in you what you see in yourself. If you feel you are unimportant, you are treated like a person who is unimportant.

To experience it do an exercise. Next time watch how a person stands while discussing with another person. You will find that many people load the entire weight of their body on one leg leaving the other leg loose. This is a wrong posture and speaks nothing good about them. A person standing on one leg projects image of a lethargic person who doesn't think of progress. This posture indicates a person who cannot be a good leader and who can't handle an important task. That is because he thinks he is unimportant. And because he feels he is unimportant, he is treated like a person who is unimportant.

In contrast, a person standing straight promises progress. See that the weight of your body is equally distributed on both the legs and your posture is straight while standing. This posture speaks of a confident person, who promises progress and is ready to accept challenges.

Similarly a sluggish walk shows that the person is reluctant to work. It projects an image of a lethargic person. Walk a bit faster. This will give you enthusiasm and help you in day-to-day activities too. Not only this, it will also help you prepare yourself to take up challenges.

It is worth repeating, people see in you what you see in yourself. It is only natural that it is for you to decide how others should take you. If you feel important, people treat you as an important person. Destroy fear and see change in the behaviour of others towards you.

Practise the following

1. Don't be a backbencher. Be a front seater.
2. Participate in every meeting. Ask questions. Make suggestions.
3. Don't avoid making eye contact. Aim your eyes direct in the eyes of others.
4. Maintain the correct postures while carrying out any activity.

□

Each person is a very good combination of pluses and minuses. Discover your pluses and be a winner.

Recognise Your Strengths

Yes...it is important, because you are the person to project yourself before the world. People see in you what you see in yourself. You will agree that you can achieve the goal set by you more easily; than the goal set by others. Therefore it is for you to decide, where you want to be.

Look around you, and you will find that thousands of people begin their career at low levels and they end up as mediocre. Not because they don't have the capability. You will find that many of them have the intellect. In some cases you will find that they are far better than others. What made them remain, where they are, is possibly they could not recognise their own strengths.

There are very few who rise faster than others, and reach the top. Not because they have extraordinary talent, but because they have sold themselves. They were convinced, they could handle higher responsibilities. "If you think you can do it, you will. If you think you can't, you will not."

There is no example in history telling us that an army that was doubtful about victory won the battle. When the troops go to the front, the soldiers undergo sessions, where confidence, courage and will power to win are pumped into them. "You think of victory, you win. Think of defeat, you lose."

Mr. Patrick Thomas worked for a dyestuff company as a sales executive. He was a good worker, who achieved his targets almost every year. In recognition he won several awards and some yearly increments. But for full eight years he remained, where he was. He was happy and content, as he never thought of anything big. He was satisfied with the small marginal increments, which he received every year along with a beautiful letter of praise.

It was only a social get together, where he met two of his friends that changed his thinking process. All of them were once classmates, and had started their career more or less at the same time and nearly the same level. One of them was AGM in a leading corporate house, and the other one had risen to the level of a 'Zonal Head'.

That day Mr. Thomas thought deeply. He sat for hours together to honestly introspect. He compared himself with his two friends. He decided to make a comparative study on a scale having several assets that he considered necessary for advancement. He strained his brain extra hard to think about those assets and finally listed them. They were as below:

- ❖ Intellect.
- ❖ General knowledge.
- ❖ Health.
- ❖ Educational qualifications.

As these friends were once classmates, he knew that they were just as good at studies, as Mr. Thomas was. They picked up the lessons and understood them just as fast as Mr. Thomas did. They did not excel on the health front either. Extra curricular activities didn't count much in the kind of job, they were in. When he did not find any remarkable difference in any of the departments he became restless. He again scribbled the same points on a sheet, but couldn't reach any conclusion.

He started giving stress to his brain to produce more points on which he could compare himself. He found two more points. 'Self-confidence and initiative.'

In these two departments he found that they really excelled. He found that the level of self-confidence had helped them in setting their goal and achieving it. The second was initiative.

Once you have identified your goal, your brain starts working in that direction and you start preparing yourself. You equip yourself to achieve your goal. Your thought process equips you for the target set by you. It never helps you in arming yourself for the goal set by others. **"Plan little, be satisfied with little. Plan big and achieve big".**

The introspection was enough for Mr. Thomas to chalk out a plan for his future. He immediately came into action. Today Mr. Thomas is a Regional Head.

Look around you, and you will find that most of the people lack confidence. When you tell them about your big plans, or tell them about your new venture, most of your friends will try to convince you, why you can't do it. Not because they are not your well-wishers. But they have a mental block. In their thinking process threats overshadow the opportunities. They find it easier to convince you why you can't succeed in competition. The repetition of negative thoughts creates a very healthy atmosphere for you to be convinced that you can't succeed. Our brain is an amazing instrument. You repeat a false statement ten times, and you find you have started believing it. As a result you give up even before starting. Thus by taking advice from 'negative thinkers' you allow a great idea to die even before it is born.

There is yet another type of advisor around you. These advisors haven't really accomplished anything measurable in their lives because of their negative thinking. As they haven't achieved anything, they naturally don't want you to rise. Such type of people will always try to pull you down to their level. They are secretly jealous of those who are successful. If you seek advice from these people, they will say something like...*nowadays there is so much competition in this field that there is hardly any scope for newcomers.* Or something like...*there are already so many people on the top, and therefore there is virtually no place for people like you.*

If you try to probe, you will discover that they hardly have any achievement to their credit.

In stark contrast, if you consult a person who has reached the top, and seek his guidance, he will not only encourage you, but also assure you of his help whenever sought. Because he knows, it can be done.

Now whom would you follow?

Those who are trying to pull you down? Or those who show you how to do it?

To do any thing we must first believe, it can be done.

Prolonged association with negative people makes us think negatively. Close contact with successful people develops habit to think positive.

Believe it can be done. This is basic truth. **"To do anything we must first believe it can be done."** This will develop confidence, and will set your mind in motion to find the way to do it.

Study a fellow who is shuffling down in mediocrity. He believes he is worth little, so he receives little. He thinks, he is unable to do big things, and naturally he doesn't. Though deep inside discontent, he pretends to be fully satisfied with little things. He believes, he is unimportant, so everything he does carries an unimportant mark. And since people see in us what we see in ourselves, he grows smaller in the estimation of others around him.

Now imagine an interesting situation, which shows a natural way of human behaviour. Imagine you come across an ad. in a newspaper showing 'Situations Vacant'. The ad. shows vacancies for two levels. Applications called for the post of 'Sales Executive' and 'Sales Manager'. Now despite having the qualities and the qualifications of a Manager, you decide to apply for the post of Sales Executive and you receive a call letter.

People see in you.
what you see in yourself.

When you walk into the office for an interview, everyone sitting in the office, right from the receptionist to other contenders (almost everyone), takes you as an Executive. The employers sitting across the table also take you as an Executive. They want to see the Executive within you, because that is what has been produced by you. Their watchful eyes try to see the Executive, which has been produced. They don't try to see the Manager hidden inside, as it has not been projected.

While sitting in the reception no one will come to you saying that you better apply for the post of 'Sales Manager', because we see a Manager hidden inside you. For that you will have to produce the Manager within you. **"People see in you, what you see in yourself."**

A study shows that there are at least 50 times more applications for low level jobs compared to the upper slots. And for key positions? There are very few. It clearly shows that there is less competition for the higher responsibilities. This sounds absurd. But it is true. This clearly indicates that there are very few people, who think progressive. It is not surprising then, that only a few reach the top. **The real leaders are in fact in short supply.** "These are the people, who believe in themselves." They believe, they can do wonders, and they do.

To accomplish big success the first condition is "you must first believe it can be done." This positive thought will develop confidence and will set your mind in motion to find the way to do it.

There will be people who will discourage you, try to drag you back, or even laugh at you. Such time is "real testing time". If you surrender to negative thoughts and succumb to the negative pressures created by the so-called well-wishers (and that is what they want), you will not be able to break the ice.

Failure is nothing more than a 'milestone' in one's life. There is no successful person who hasn't seen failures. Failures are in one way necessary, because they make you strong.

Tough times, hardships, failures are only the milestones to show you, how far you are from your goal. If you start gasping and sit there holding the milestone, cursing the hard luck or bad luck, you will gain nothing, but will only lose the clear vision of the goal. Sit at the milestone for a while, and make a self-review. Try to find out where things went wrong and what needs to be corrected. An honest introspection will help you find a better way to reach the target. Make sure, the failure doesn't shake your self-confidence, because if your confidence is shaken, you may tend to think, the target is beyond your reach.

At failures try to think of those successful people who haven't seen failures, and you will discover there is none.

The only thing they carried along was courage. They never lost confidence, and always believed, they could do it and they did.

To accomplish anything it is important that "you don't underestimate yourself". If you ever try to go in for a post-mortem and analyse failure, you will find that in most cases wrong self-assessment is the main cause. Quite often we underestimate ourselves and overestimate others.

And there is an interesting co-relation. The moment you overestimate others, you automatically become smaller in your own estimation. The more you overestimate others, the more you grow smaller. And as people see in you, what you see in yourself, it becomes more important how you 'assess' yourself.

Feel Important

As a human being everyone wants respect. And there is nothing wrong in it, because respect determines one's size. If you want others to respect you, it is necessary that you respect yourself first. To have respect from others you must have respect for yourself first. If you feel you are important, others will feel you are important too.

What kind of feelings do you carry for a person who shows by his actions that he is inferior and unimportant? The answer is obvious. He is not respected because the poor guy himself feels he is unimportant. And because he feels unimportant, everything that he does carries an unimportant mark. The result is that the poor guy does not get the treatment, he probably deserves.

To gain respect of others, you must first believe you deserve respect. And the more respect you have for yourself, the more respect others will have for you. It is worth repeating: *we receive the kind of treatment we think we deserve.*

Because how we think determines our act. And how we act in turn determines how others react to us.

To feel important it is necessary to look important.

How you look on the outside,
affects how you feel
on the inside.

Look Important

We have been hearing the great 'philosophy' of simple living and high thinking. It sounds great. We also say that a person should be judged by his intellect and not by his appearance. The statement is pleasant, but look at the other side of it. It is true that we have examples of many successful people and great leaders who believed in the 'philosophy' of simple living and high thinking, and also led a life of simple living successfully. But it cannot be laid down as a thumb rule. The reason is very simple. One needs a moderately long period of time to prove his mettle. In the first place the bitter truth is that he can do so only if given a chance. And he will get a chance only if his appearance supports him. Today people judge a person by his appearance.

"Yes. It is true". Your appearance talks. It talks a lot about you. It talks to you, and it talks to others as well.

To understand how your appearance talks to you, look at it this way. Your appearance regulates your thinking. Have you ever noticed how beautifully and how carefully people choose their clothes before going to a social get-together? How colourfully ladies are dressed? They do so because it gives them confidence. This confidence can be seen in their actions. This is why we say, your appearance talks to you. "Your physical exterior affects your mental interior". If you are sure about appearance, you feel confident. It makes you feel important. Your actions show it. "How you look on the outside, affects how you feel on the inside".

Now when we say, your appearance talks to others,

we mean it. How do you feel about a person who comes to an important event in a dirty shirt, his shoes are not polished, beard not shaved off and moustache not trimmed? Do you think anyone would respect him? Obviously not, because the person makes a poor impression. The appearance of this fellow speaks nothing good about him. It tells people that here is a person who is lazy, careless, inefficient and unimportant. Because of these qualities he deserves no special consideration.

In stark contrast, a well-dressed person conveys many positive things. His appearance tells people that this is a person who is important. He thinks progressive, and is dependable.

When a person enters a new place, people often make a quick assessment about him in their subconscious mind and then treat him accordingly. For this they don't have to try, but this is a spontaneous act. In today's competitive environment special emphasis is given on packaging in addition to quality of the product. Have you noticed how only a few shops attract you in the vegetable market or fruit market, while others selling the same vegetables or fruits don't? Not only this, they also command a better price. This is because of their way of presentation. The same product commands a better price when packaged attractively. Appearance is that important.

A shabby looking person is not respected because his appearance says many negative things about him. A well-dressed person feels confident, and hence feels important.

This feeling regulates his actions, and his actions in turn determine how others treat him.

Next time when you are going on a mission, leave home only after you make sure, you look the kind of person, you want to be. Make sure, your appearance reflects only positive things about you. See that your appearance suits the occasion. **And don't be misled. Good appearance doesn't necessarily mean expensive clothes or costly shoes. Don't worry if you do not have expensive dresses. Even frugal attire can make a good dress, and can add value to your appearance, provided it shows good taste and suits the occasion.** Only you must make sure, it is not dirty. Ensure your dress is clean and your shoes are polished. This will make you feel important, and will help you think positively about yourself. Also this positive thinking will naturally regulate your actions, and will tell others that they can't afford to size you down.

Practise the following

- Look for reasons why you can do it, and not why you can't.
- Think you can win, and you will.
- Seek advice only from successful people. Never consult negative thinkers.
- Believe in yourself. Don't underestimate yourself and overestimate others.
- Accept failures and learn from them. There is no successful person, who hasn't seen failures.

- Feel important. Look at your pluses instead of looking at your minuses. This will give you confidence.
- Have respect for yourself, and you will find that others have respect for you too.
- Take care of your appearance. Next time when you leave home, make sure, you look like the person you want to be.

□

Keep Your Attitude Positive

One's attitude plays a crucial role in his or her progress. What is the meaning of attitude? Or how does the positive attitude help us?

Mr. S.J. was working in a company where I worked for a few years. He had spent a pretty long period of his life working in the same position. He worked for upward of 30 years. He would come to the office and do his routine work without any efforts to see whether he could do something more productive. Whenever someone would approach him with some additional work, one could easily see him frown. His first reaction would be a spontaneous unpleasant grimace, an unpleasant reluctant look on his face. He would tell through gestures that you are expecting something extra (other than his duty) from him. No wonder then that he retired as a billing clerk, the post where he came thirty years ago.

One is unable to work is one thing, but one does not want to work is another thing. Someone willing to work but not delivering results may have justifications, and may be helped, because he has put-in genuine efforts. There are all chances that the fellow will do better, if given proper guidance and a chance. But not willing to work is an attitude problem. I have seen people who prefer to spend more time in convincing their seniors why they can't do a particular job, than the time required to finish it. The fact is that they may finish it off in less than half the time they spend for convincing others why they can't do it.

Some people work because they have to, because they need salary. Others work for advancement. Some people have the "I have done my duty and that's enough" attitude. These people kill their valuable time in gossiping about the company's annual increments. They talk about the company's superannuation policy. You can often find them talking about the company's profits, but they do not bother themselves to think how the company's profits can go up, and how they can contribute towards this goal. These people are more concerned with what the company is doing for them, but never try to see what they are doing for the company.

But those with a positive attitude don't waste their time in thinking what the company is doing for them. They fruitfully spend their time in planning how they can contribute to the company's betterment. Such people always try to ensure that they do something better with every coming day. Organisations are working for progress. They need people who dream progress. It is natural that organisations thrive on such people, and these are the people who move up the ladder.

Do you read body language? Believe it; you can easily read one's attitude. It shows through one's actions. **What we think shows through how we act.** Next time when you board an aeroplane, try to read the gestures of the air hostesses; and you will know which one has fixed an artificial 'plastic smile' on her face and which one welcomes the fellow passengers from inside; from the depth of the heart.

It is difficult; No.... it is rather impossible for a person to conceal his real feelings. This is why we say: "What you think, shows through how you act". Attitudes can't be hidden. Positive or negative, they can be read by others.

You don't need to know the language to say you are in love. Your eyes will do it for you. You need no words to say you like someone or you don't like someone. You don't have to say you admire someone or you hate someone. To read one's face or to study one's body language is easier than we think. And we do it every day. Knowingly or unknowingly, in our conscious or subconscious mind, we always read minds.

Remember: others also read our mind like we read others'. It is equally easy for them to read our mind like it is for us.

There are absolutely no chances for anyone to find a person, who has a negative attitude and yet has achieved something big. Achievers essentially have a big asset with them, and that is 'Positive Attitude'.

While at the workplace try to learn as much as you can, may be outside of your daily routine work. Don't keep the 'I have done my job' attitude. The more you learn, the faster you grow. Don't see what the company is doing for you. Try to see what you can do for the company.

Enlarge your orbit. If you are working in production, try to learn something about marketing. So you will get to know about the difficulties marketing people have to face while marketing the products made by you. You will know what sort of complaints they are confronted with, day in and day out in the market place. It will help you improve the quality of the product.

If you are working in the sales department, try to learn something about production, or may be 'Costing'. It will help you know what the problems of those people are, and why you are not getting the quality of a product that you are expecting.

Try to take-up more responsibility. Never take any additional work as an 'unpleasant load'. Never try to shirk off any additional responsibility just because it is not your job. Remember… you have to take up more responsibilities as you go high. The higher you go, the more responsible you are. The following diagram will show how your job profile changes with every step upward.

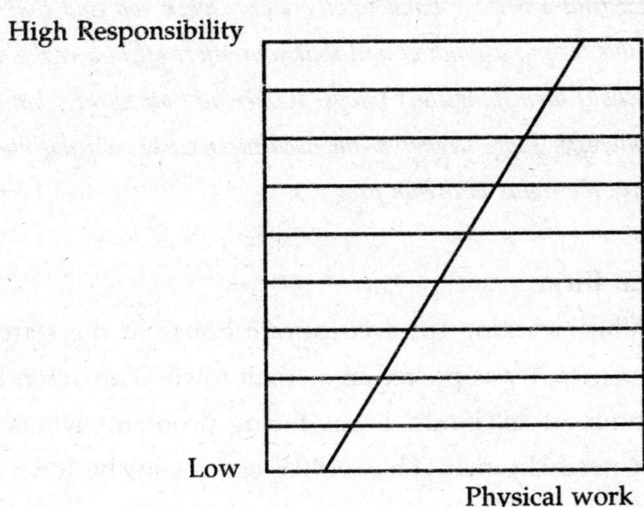

You will notice how you do less physical work but become more responsible with every step upward.

Here it is important to know that taking additional responsibilities **does not mean** interfering in other's business or poking nose into other departments even when not needed. This kind of act may embarrass others. Often it is seen that some over ambitious people try unnecessarily to interfere in the areas that are not related to them. **Some people do it just to shift the attention of others from their mistakes, so that their own weaknesses may be obscured.** This type of act is ostensibly to help their colleagues but secretly to overshadow them. In many cases it is found that these people are not honest to their own job, neither doing justice to it, but are always ready with their suggestions for others.

Extend a helping hand to others only when you find that they are unable to find a solution and that your effort offers a real sincere help without tarnishing their image. Remember; others also have the same interests, same strengths and weaknesses like you do, and as such have the rights to dream progress.

Service First

While working for a corporate house in the state of Maharashtra, I was posted in a small town. This town had limitations of all kinds. I was facing problems whenever my car needed repair. The service centres in the town did not maintain inventory of spares, as the sale was limited. They would place an order for high priced spares when an urgent requirement would arise.

Further the town didn't have too many competent mechanics. Each time my car needed a repair, I had to wait for weeks. To avoid this problem, I was on the look for a mechanic who maintained an inventory of all the spares and who had an expert hand.

One Sunday morning while going on a long trip, I saw a glow signboard of a service centre. I pulled up my car outside to see whether it was the one, I was looking for. I got down and went up to the counter, where a neatly dressed person welcomed me with a pleasant genuine smile. This was the owner of the centre. While discussing with him, I saw that two of his attendants were busy cleaning my car. Within ten minutes they had removed the entire dust from the windscreen, window glasses and other visible parts. When

I got back to my car, I realised how dirty it was before I came here. What really impressed me was that he expected nothing in return. In the coming days, I noticed that it was the regular practice at this service centre. As soon as a car pulled up outside his service centre, his men would start removing dust from it to make sure, it looked clean. They did it with every vehicle, whether a regular customer or a casual visitor.

This gesture really impressed me. Next time when my car needed servicing, this was the only place where I could expect the best. And of course I was not wrong. After a few visits to this garage I realised that this man had a real sincere willingness to offer the best he could.

It was not surprising then that within months it became the first choice of the car owners. I also noticed that no one did ever have to repent for going there. It had to become the leading service centre, and it actually did.

Money is a great power. You need money for every thing that you want to do. If you want to give your wife and children a better standard of living, you need money. If you want to help those, who you feel are deprived, but deserve a better education; or if you wish to help those poor children in orphanages who have no rays of hope in their life, you need money. At every step you need money. You can't move a step forward without it. But while it is true, it is equally true and equally important that you can't reap the harvest of money unless you have sown the seeds of it. And you can do it by giving service first.

In the above case, I found that the service centre people could have given me a routine treatment, because I was not till then a regular customer for them. But the centre owner did not think of it that way. When I visited this centre the first time, he sowed the seeds of money.

"Put the service first" attitude helps you in all the situations. In the early years of my professional career, I worked for a few years with a man whom I'll call Mr. SK. This guy was a classic case study of its kind. SK had a different kind of attitude. Before handing out any thing he always thought what he would get in return. He however wanted others to discuss his financial problems, which he always had. A father of four children, he always ran short of funds. He was convinced (and tried to convince others) that he was the most underpaid employee in the company. He always pleaded that the company should pay him more because his bills were getting larger, while the salary cheque wasn't. He spent hours while on duty, telling others how badly he needed more money. But he never spent time in thinking how he could get more money.

When he found his name was dropped by the company from the list of those considered for an annual increment, he was furious. He dashed open the door of the Divisional Manager's cabin and stormed into it. For about half an hour we could only guess what must have been happening inside. The clatter coming out made it clear that it was a fray and not a story telling, that was in progress inside the closed doors.

When he came out, he was all heated-up. Anger blazed in his eyes. It was clear that the decision taken by the management was final and for a salary raise he would have to wait for at least a year.

While his colleagues had sympathy for him, no one was convinced with the reasons given by him for a raise. When I overheard his reaction, I was wondering how this man could expect a salary raise with such baseless reasons. Look at some of his remarks: "Mr. X has been given a very good raise despite the fact that he has only recently got married, and has no children to look after". "He doesn't need even half the money that I need. And when I told the Manager about my urgent need for money, that callous person told me that let your work prove you need more money. That grump thinks that I will work harder for a raise. Only a fool will do that."

Now while SK needed more money, he should have proved it through his work. His plea that he would work harder only if the company paid him more doesn't really help, because the system doesn't work that way. People don't get a raise on promising to work. They get a raise only after producing results.

'Service first' attitude is really greater than it sounds. You can reap greater volumes only if you offer your sincere service without expecting any returns. An entrepreneur invests money in business. Other expenditures may return dividends or may not, but investment of this kind does. The condition is it should be done without expecting any returns.

"Offer the best you can, money will take care of itself."

Respect your job

It has been found that there is a close co-relation between one's job respect and job performance. Ask yourself whether you feel pride in carrying out your day-to-day work? If the answer is yes, there is no reason why you can't deliver results. In fact there are all chances that you must be delivering much more than expected from you. Look around you and try to study. You will invariably find that those who do not feel pride about their job or their company must be those who never do justice with their job and never deliver results.

A few years ago, while travelling I met a salesman who represented a company involved in the business of switchgears and cables. When asked about his job, he introduced himself as a poor fellow with low competence. He considered himself a downtrodden and deprived person who was being sucked by the company. He clearly had no respect for the company. Neither had he any respect for his job. While the fellow thought he was underpaid, I believed he didn't even deserve what he was getting. Persons having such an attitude are never effective performers. They are respected neither by their seniors, nor in the market place. The reason is simple. Those who are in close contact with them know well that such people are never honest to anyone, because they are not honest to themselves.

In yet another similar situation a salesman introduced

himself as a person who brought revenue. Have a look at the words he used for his job. When asked about his job profile, he said, "I am carrying out the most important function for my organisation." I bring revenue which is the most important power to run the show. I earn profits for my company. I did not have any doubts about the success of this fellow. The reason was simple. He had respect for his job. Not only this. The way he described his job, I'm sure he must have moved many stairs upwards.

Remember, what you do is only as important as you feel. It is therefore very significant to know that **how you do is as important as what you do.** Never have the feeling that you are doing something unimportant. This negative thought will make you uncomfortable, and will affect your performance. Feel pride about your job. Display pride for the company you are working for. Start looking at the positive side of your job. This will fill new enthusiasm in you, which will work as a catalyst and pave your way for further growth.

Treat the company problem as your own problem. You will notice that those who have been picked-up by the company for higher responsibilities have always shown their concern for their company. I have found that often companies create new slots for such people, because they can't afford losing them. Work shirkers are respected nowhere. Whenever one of your colleagues is picked-up by the management for a higher responsibility, there is resentment amongst those coveting a promotion. Co-workers start saying many negative things. Many stories are made to prove that he has been given something, he does not deserve.

Put your foot into the shoes of your senior and imagine what you would have done if you were in his place. Whom would you have promoted if you had the responsibility of your senior? If you ask yourself these questions with full sincerity, the answer will definitely endorse his decision.

Often I have seen that those holding higher responsibilities are watchful for their successor, especially when heading towards retirement. In fact they have to be vigilant, as they have the responsibility of grooming their successor, so that they can smoothly hand over their charge to him and rest assured. This is a time-consuming and sensitive exercise, as any mistake at this level may prove expensive. In most cases, I have found that the first choice of the management is a person who owns responsibilities and doesn't shirk them off. And the reason is simple. In such situations only a person can succeed who treats company problems as his own personal problems. You can easily find people having sleepless nights when there is a disorder in a machine and the production is at standstill. These are the people who display the attitude that is necessary for the growth of the organisation, and of course necessary for their individual growth.

Practise the following:

1. Start taking additional responsibilities.
2. Enlarge your orbit. Take interest in learning something other than your routine job.

3. Put the service first attitude.
4. Have respect for your job.
5. Treat company problems as your own problems.

Remember: what we think shows through how we act. Keep the attitude positive and you'll find that the doors of success are opening for you.

□

Ensure Your Environment is Clean

A few years ago, I came across a news article in a 'local daily' which narrated a case of the assassination of a lady. People were shocked when they knew that the lady's nephew was apprehended by the cops. The cops suspected him, not because he pointed a clue, but because of the company he kept. He often flocked with the 'street corner bum' sort of boys who did nothing but only killed time teasing the school-going girls.

It was only when the real culprits were caught, that the police discovered, that the victim's nephew was innocent. The police suspected him only because of the company he kept, the environment he lived in.

Remember, you are judged by the company you keep. Have you ever noticed how we keep a 'Rat-Kill' or a body poison in the upper shelf to keep it out of children's reach? And it is good that we do it. Because we know that it may cause great damage.

There is yet another poison which may damage to a greater degree. The 'thought poison'. What makes it more harmful is that the person doesn't know that he is consuming it.

You are a product of your environment. What you are today is a result of your earlier environment, 5-10-15 years back. Similarly your today's environment will decide what you will be 5 or 10 years from now. Try to study some typical habits of those around you. You will find that most of their habits have been influenced by somebody. Look at some of their relatively unimportant habits, and you will know what kind of company they keep. The way a person walks, the way he speaks, his choice of words, the way he holds his cup of tea, everything will tell you about his company.

You have all types of people around you. All are not alike. Some are positive, some are negative. Name a place where you don't find negators. They are everywhere, in your society, in schools, at working places—everywhere. In your office you will find that different people have different attitudes. Some work because they have to work. Others work for advancement. Some people always have their eyes on the clock. You will find that these are the people who are steeped in mediocrity throughout their lives.

On the first day at your workplace you will have many well-wishers who will come forward to help you. But don't be misled. Quite often you will find that all the advices that you get are not worth accepting. Some 'free lance advisors' may tell you something like "the best way to get-along here is confine yourself to your work". Or to be comfortable don't show that you have free time. Beware of your boss. "Don't show him that you have finished your work even if you have". "Otherwise he will load you down".

Now think for a while. If the advice of these people were right, they would have been handling big responsibilities. But you will find that these people remain till the last working day of their professional life, where they had joined 25 years ago.

It is obvious, taking advice from such well-wishers will never steer your way to higher grades. Such friends will never endorse you if you try to learn more, learn fast. They feel uncomfortable if they find that you are sincerely trying to take-up on more work and learn more. This is because deep inside they know that by taking interest in things other than your job, you will outshine, which they don't want. Such people always want to pull you down to their level. They shuffle down in mediocrity throughout their lives. And they want you to do it too.

To experiment tell them about your great plans. You will find that they laugh at you. Tell them "my ambition is to become 'General Manager' of this company". What do you think will be their reaction? First of all they will think you are joking, and will make stories out of it. Perhaps they will try to console you pleading that it is foolish to even think that way. Possibly they will try to convince you that you need big contacts to reach the top.

Now imagine for a while, you repeat the same statement with equal sincerity to the president of your company. How do you think he will react? One thing is certain. He will not laugh. Because he knows it is possible. **Big people do not laugh at big ideas.** On the contrary, he will try to find if your statement was made with full sincerity. If he finds you mean it, he will guide you and will try to groom you to ensure that you prepare yourself for higher responsibilities.

Those who tell you something cannot be done are almost always the people who are 'unsuccessful'. Their negative attitude is the only reason for their failure. And since they could not do it, they don't want you to do it too.

Study negators. Be extra careful while choosing your friends. "Taking advice from negative thinking people reduces the size of your thinking". Keep close contact with those who are successful. It will generate ambition in you.

Recall your school days. How a student trying sincerely to attain a position in the top ranks was jeered at. He often became a subject of jokes for some students. But those who knew how harmful it was to have such friends, kept far from such company.

May it be a school, or may it be a workplace. There are always some people who make the environment unhealthy, and an unhealthy environment can never inspire you to dream success.

Have you noticed *why certain things are said quite loudly in the presence of all, while some statements are whispered only after making sure no one overhears?* This is because the one, who whispers, knows his statement is a hundred per cent false.

He has a guilt feeling.

We must be smart enough to distinguish between an honest statement and gossip. Gossip is often baseless and comes out of jealousy. This is why such statements are generally whispered. And the person involved in gossip makes sure, no one overhears. Also if the subject suddenly comes in, the person making the statement about him fails to look into his eyes.

Talk about people. Even in their absence. But stay on the positive side. Remember, no one is perfect. You will find many good qualities in a person if you sincerely try to find them.

Above all, you lose the faith of your seniors very fast if you continue to flock with people having negative thinking. So make sure you take advice only from those, who believe in progress, those who breathe success. It will inspire you to dream of big accomplishments.

Be extra careful while making friends. Ensure that your environment is clean.

□

Achievers are no different people. They are just human beings like you.

Small Habits that Matter

In day-to-day activities there are occasions when some habits that appear comparatively unimportant, matter a lot. These habits make a difference. These habits determine how others take us, as these are the acts, which create impressions about us. Also these are the habits, which sooner or later make us realise what we should have done and what we missed.

Time Management

We all know the meaning of Time Management and its importance. Time Management simply means best utilisation of available time.

I often come across people who think and claim that they use more than 70 per cent of the day effectively. Now honestly speaking, you can't do it, even if you sincerely want. For you don't have more than 66 per cent of your lifetime to do it. "Sounds absurd". Doesn't it?

Look at it this way. We all know that there are 24 hours in a day. Now take a note of your routine from one morning to the next one. While observing all that you do, see how much time you spend in bed. You will find that it is somewhere between 7 to 8 hours. And even medical science suggests that a healthy person needs sound sleep of 7 to 8 hours a day. It means that a person maintaining average health spends a third of his day in bed. "By this token a person living a life of 75 years spends upwards of 25 years in bed". Sounds unbelievable. But it is true. This ratio of 1 over 2 will be further higher in case of those who are often sick or maintain indifferent health. Now looking at the fact that we spend a third of our lifetime in bed doing nothing creative, how much is left for us? The answer is obvious. Not more than 66 per cent.

When we find that we hardly have two thirds of our lifetime to be used creatively, it becomes all the more important to use this time smartly. It is foolish to think, we can stretch a day to 28 hours from 24. And it is not sensible to shrink the sleeping time as well, as this will directly affect our efficiency. We all know how a tired person, who hasn't had sound sleep, works. What is the solution then?

Mr. Irwin was an ambitious person, and sincerely wanted to make progress in life. To ensure faster growth he wanted to have a professional degree in finance. But after his father's death, was forced to accept a low profile job of maintaining accounts in a Super Market after completion of a degree in commerce. He felt restless, but couldn't help it, as his job gave him no time for studies. A full time course was a dream for him, as earning for the family was a compulsion.

He would be dead tired when he was back at home after a day's work. But he was one of those, who surrender to the goal.

He found that he could sacrifice two hours that he spent with friends for refreshing, and could reduce the time given for dinner and other unimportant activities. He also knew well, it was the need of the hour, and that this sacrifice would pave his way to new heights. Irwin was smart enough to reschedule his daily routine. He joined night classes for guidance. Stretched a little extra hard for two years. Today he heads the accounts department of a medium-sized company.

We know well, we can't stretch the length of the day, or we can't add days to a year. They will remain the same. What we can do is, see where we can save time and what are those unimportant activities that waste or fritter away our time. Once you identify these areas, you will find it easier to use these 'extra' hours for a purposeful task.

Look for Simple Solutions

Long ago, in a training programme, in which I was also a participant, the faculty told us a fictitious tale. I repeat the story here, which goes like this.

A father, while going along with his son on a motorbike, met with an accident. The father died on the spot and the son was seriously injured. He was immediately rushed to the nearby hospital. His wounds needed immediate operation, so he was moved to the operation theatre. But as soon as the doctor saw the patient, the doctor said, "Oh my god, he is my son, I can't operate on him."

After finishing the story the faculty asked a question to the participants. How is that possible?

All the participants started scratching their heads. After about two minutes' silence the answers started pouring in. Someone said, "The son had a similar looking fellow", who confused the doctor. One participant said he had a twin brother. Each one had a new idea. Many were of the opinion that the doctor was lying. Some of the answers are not worth repeating here.

After about ten minutes' brainstorming session the correct answer came. And the correct answer was "the doctor was the patient's mother". The answer was much simpler than the congregation thought. *The purpose of telling the story however was not clear to any one of us, as the message hidden was not clear.*

After a pause the faculty asked us two questions.

1. Why can't we look for simple solutions? And
2. Why we can't expect a lady to be a doctor

Now the message was very clear. We often complicate matters and multiply the problems, whereas most of the times simple solutions are available. **Also it is often seen that some people are impressed only if and only when they find a solution, which is difficult to be understood, and which comes out after immense struggle.**

Do you remember a very popular story of a toothpaste company that was facing a problem in the market? The story tells us how the company was desperately trying to increase the sales that were dwindling. The company reviewed its publicity campaign and tried to see if there was a problem in packaging. They didn't find any problem in the quality either. Everything was in line but the sales continued to dwindle. At last the solution came, which was much simpler than anybody ever thought.

The solution was hidden in the design of the tube. The company changed it and increased the diameter of the outlet of the toothpaste tube. When the consumer opened the tube and applied the paste on the bristles, it spread more quantity of the paste. Each time the consumer would consume more quantity of the paste. And if one consumed fast, one would purchase fast. This simple solution helped to increase the sales.

Never forget that the majority of people in a group have an average understanding. You can't expect every person to have extraordinary intellect. They need simple solutions to the problems, so that a smooth implementation can be ensured.

The second question was self-explanatory. When a lady can be a Prime Minister, or a pilot, why can't she be a doctor? Women are no longer effeminate. Today they are actively working in every field. In fact in some cases they have proved, they can be better than their male counterparts. To accept the fact, that a lady can handle a higher responsibility, we only have to accept her as a human being.

□

Importance of Timely Action

We all know the importance of time and timely action in our life. That is why we always make sure that we reach the railway station on time, so that we don't miss the train. We similarly reach the airport much before the take-off time, because we know that the airplane will not wait for us. Not only this, we also keep some cushion to meet the unforeseen situations like the traffic jam. It is good that we do it. But these are only a few examples, which show the impact of delay immediately.

There are other more important occasions in our life, when the delay in action doesn't penalise us instantly. But the damage caused may be of a greater degree. Sometimes the results of delay are seen much later. In some cases the results are seen years later. A young aspirant, who is preparing for a competitive examination, gets a lifetime penalty, if he fails to submit his forms before the due date.

To know the importance of ten years of life ask a prisoner, who has been sentenced for life imprisonment. Only a student who couldn't succeed in the annual

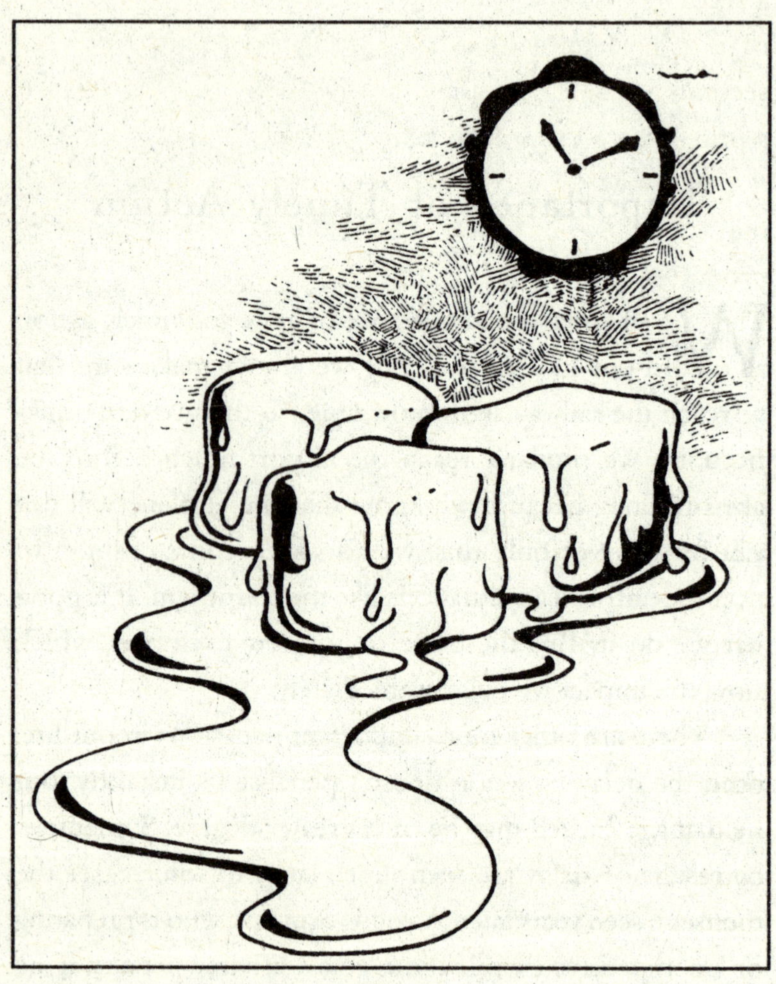

Take timely action to avoid losses

examination can tell you the importance of a year. But if you really want to know the importance of a hundredth of a second, ask the athlete who lost the title by a hundredth of a second. Sometimes delay in taking action even by a second may cost us a lifetime penalty. We may have to pay a price, which cannot be recovered in a lifetime.

An ice-vendor knows better, how important it is for him to sell his product today. Because if he doesn't sell his product today, there is nothing left for him the next day. The same applies to a vegetable vendor, and so it is with all of us.

In fact time is like a fistful of sand, which slips away from our fist without letting us stop it. We can hold the arms of a clock to a halt, but that doesn't stop the time. The sun will rise and set, whether we wish it or not.

Imagine—you have to face an important interview, which is going to decide the direction of your future. For some reason you fail to reach the place and report on time, and you are told that the management has finalised some other candidate. Such loss is a lifetime loss. Imagine what a situation it would make, if the armed forces of our enemy country attack in Kargil or Ladakh and our forces keep themselves confined to conducting meetings on our policy or on our role to ensure peace. If they squander time in discussing how and when we have to react, the chances are that instead of fighting in Kargil today, they will have to struggle in Delhi a week later.

Remember: **Today's threat may become a real crisis tomorrow.**

This is why it is important to act on a threat before it becomes a crisis. We all know that it is easier and simpler to solve a problem when it is in the budding stage. That is because it requires less effort, less energy and less time. In some cases it may require less manpower coupled with little money. But the same problem, if not solved in time, becomes a big threat, as it grows fast with time. As time passes, you eventually find yourself facing a crisis. And once it becomes a crisis, it asks for larger manpower, longer period of time and more money to get rid of it.

Do you remember the world's largest 'industrial disaster' in the known history? That was the gas leak accident in a pesticide plant in our country. The plant was owned by a multinational corporate house, and had all the 'fail safe systems' installed to ensure the safety. But the whole world saw how the deadly poisonous gas (MIC) leaked and cost lives of thousands of human beings and cattle. This was again a classic example of how dangerous (or even fatal) a delay in taking action may prove. A timely action would have brought the failure of 'fail safe systems' in the knowledge. Similarly timely switching off the production of MIC could have saved the lives of all those ill fated, who died of strangulation.

Remember: *If you don't solve a silly problem today, you 'along with your team members' will fight a big crisis tomorrow.*

Misconception about timely action

There is a misconception about timely action. We often misinterpret it. Generally an early action is 'almost always' mistaken as timely action. But timely does not always mean an early action. There is a clear-cut difference between a timely and an early action. Sounds absurd. Doesn't it?

Look at it this way. Sometimes early actions are taken in haste as a result of a 'momentary flash' of emotions. Such actions are 'premature', and the results are like 'premature deliveries', which give birth to unhealthy and underdeveloped infants. **You don't go to the examination centre a day before the examination, however strong your preparation is. Do you?**

'Drinks & Delicacies' was a leading soft drink company. Peter Joe was its Marketing Manager. He looked after the development, launch and marketing of new products. Otherwise intelligent Joe was too enthusiastic to launch the new flavour without caring that the summer was at its fag end. The new flavour was launched when the summer was about to say goodbye. Naturally the response was lukewarm.

The remaining months witnessed a rather lethargic purchase trend, as usual waiting for the next season to arrive. By the time the next summer approached, Peter Joe found that the same flavour launched by the competitors had occupied the shelves in the market place.

Here the results would have been different, if Mr. Joe had spent his time and talent for developing the packaging of the new flavour. Also he could have spent time in developing the price structure and marketing policies. Publicity was another area, which needed his attention.

We often interpret that an early action is always useful, without thinking it may lead to a premature delivery.

Decide your priorities

To make sure, your actions are fruitful, decide your 'time-bound' priorities. You will find it easier if you do it in phases. The following exercise will help you make an effective time bound action plan:

1. Fix your priorities in the year (12 months).
2. Fix your priorities in the next 6 months.
3. Fix your priorities in the next quarter.
4. Decide your priorities in the next one month.
5. Decide your priorities for the next week.
6. And finally how you have to plan your day.

A periodic review will definitely help, as slight changes can be carried out as and when required.

□

People don't plan to fail.
They fail to plan.

Identify Your Goal

What is the meaning of using goals in one's life? Why is it important? To understand it imagine a person 'P' who fills the fuel tank of his car and starts on an unknown or 'unidentified' mission. After every 10-15 minutes' drive he takes a turn, which may be right or left. Which way he chooses depends fully on his 'whims' at that particular moment. He continues his drive towards his 'unidentified' goal endlessly for a whole day. In the evening when his fuel tank is empty, he tries to locate where he has reached. Where do you think he must have reached? There are fair chances for 'Mr. P.' to find himself either at the starting point or perhaps he will find himself lost in the labyrinth of some narrow streets (near his starting point), which take him nowhere.

It is applicable to all of us. Those who achieve something big in life set their goals without fail and push themselves hard only in that direction. You will find that they don't change their goal every now and then. They surrender themselves fully to their goal to ensure, they don't rest until they achieve it.

A classmate of mine was fond of cricket. He really played well when he represented our school team. The natural appreciation that he received after every single good performance filled a little dose of cricket in his mind. It was natural that he dreamt of taking up cricket as a career. The kind of glamour, big money and fame enjoyed by cricketers overshadowed his other capabilities and prompted him to cherish dreams of becoming a big cricketer. But playing good cricket in a school team alone doesn't make one a good cricketer. It needs commitment, devotion and dedication. He often skipped classroom sessions for unimportant matches. By doing so, he shifted his focus from studies to cricket. It was only expected that he scored poorly in almost all the subjects.

This craze for cricket would still have been fruitful, if he had excelled in the sport. But at college level he found himself as a standby when the university team was formed. It was only then, that he realised that he could not make his career in cricket. A few months later when he met me, I found that he had given up the idea of being a cricketer, and began experimenting with poetry. But this field hardly had a promising career for him, as he wrote little.

While I found that there was absolutely no relation between the two fields, he was still hopeful, as he received some sort of appreciation for a few poems that he wrote for children.

Then I didn't hear anything about him, as I left the

town for my career. A long period of about ten years went past. And suddenly one fine evening I saw him in a fair price shop. This time I found a totally different person in him. His dreams and ambitions had long since faded. Cricket and poetry had gone into oblivion. He was completely lost. He looked tired of life. With his wife and two children he found it hard to make ends meet. It was apparent that life had become a burden for him.

Now where do you think things went wrong? This true story can be a classic case study of wrong planning. "In the first place his self-assessment was wrong". He should have seen his potential and his capabilities. Probably he wouldn't have reached this condition, had he sincerely looked at his own potential, capabilities and then chosen his goal.

In the second place, instead of surrendering to his goal he kept changing his goals every now and then, only to find himself lost in the labyrinth of dark streets of life. He groped for a ray of hope, but instead faced the bitter truth of life.

Remember: People don't plan to fail. They fail to plan.

How to set your goal

You will agree that every individual has some pluses and some minuses. Therefore it is natural that each one of us have certain limitations. If you know your strengths and weaknesses well, you will more effectively set your goal. A good cine-star enjoying big money, glamour and fame may fascinate anyone. But to become a successful cine-star it is necessary to have an inclination towards acting. Merely thinking of becoming a big actor doesn't help any one become a great star.

It is therefore important to set your goal carefully. To successfully achieve the target set by you, the first and foremost thing, that is important, is that **"The target must be achievable".**

At the very first glance if the target seems 'unachievable', it is 100 per cent certain that the target is not set to be achieved. If you are asked to leave Delhi and reach New York within two hours, the message is simple and clear, that you don't have to try. While setting the goal, see that it is achievable; else you will give up even before you start chasing it.

While the goal should be achievable, it doesn't mean that it should be achievable effortlessly. The reason is very simple. If you know, something can be achieved effortlessly; you are not likely to make efforts. When there are no efforts, there are no chances for any improvement. And complacency is the biggest hurdle in one's progress. You will agree that life is meaningless if one doesn't improve and enrich oneself with every passing day.

So try to stretch your capabilities, and set your goal keeping your limitations in mind. **Your ideal goal is the one, which needs your concentrated efforts and your capabilities stretched to their maximum.**

Now what puts you in motion is 'time limit'. No goal can be achieved without setting a time-bound action plan. Again, like achievability, this 'time limit' should also be set smartly.

You will notice that in business organisations the 'Sales Managers' are given a well-defined quota, which is carefully and skilfully distributed among the sales persons, looking at their previous performance and the future potential. They have to achieve the targets set for them within a given time-limit, and a well-defined territory. Without this they will run directionless wasting their time.

While setting your goal, see that it takes you in a direction, which fulfils your dream. Surrender fully to the goal set by you. Unless you do it, it has no value. Make sure that **"Today's dream is tomorrow's reality".** Your today's dream will remain a dream without a proper 'work-plan'. There is a clear-cut difference between a 'dream' and an 'aim'. Your dream will come true only if acted upon.

Accept failures—We hate failures. We want success in everything that we do. While it is true that success pleases us, it is also true that sometimes we may have to face failures. Look around you. Look at those, you consider most successful persons, and you will find that almost all of them have seen failures. Try to study and you will find that they learnt what went wrong and took corrective steps.

To understand it better, suppose you are going to a certain place 'A' and reach a situation where the road is blocked. What do you do? You don't camp there. Neither you drop the idea of going to the place 'A' and decide to go to another place 'B'. When you discover that this way will not take you where you want to go, you take another way. You certainly don't change your target. Despite knowing that a particular way will not take you where you want to go, if you continue your journey on the same way, you will reach nowhere.

People searching for ground water, bore well, but when they don't find a source of water, they don't go to ridiculous depths. They try at a new place. The only thing, they stay with, is their goal.

Stay with your goal. Let your dream be your goal.

Day-to-day planning is important

The following exercise will help you in effective planning.

1. Plan what you want to be 5 years from now.
2. Plan what you want to do in the next one year.
3. Plan your work in the next 6 months.
4. Divide your 6 months' plan in 2 parts. First 3 months and second 3 months.
5. Make your plan for the next 3 months.
6. Decide your priorities for the next 1 month.
7. Plan your work for the day, keeping in view your month's plan.

Have you noticed the difference between a Sunday and a working day? How wastefully sometimes a Sunday passes by? The reason is very simple. Quite often we don't chalk out a plan for a Sunday. Very often we rise late on Sundays. We waste another hour sipping tea or coffee and gossiping lethargically. Take a bath when the sun is at its peak. Take a siesta after a late lunch even if not necessary. Go for a long drive in the evening, and finally go to bed when the day is over. The same day is better used in a creative way, or in finishing some pending jobs, if planned on the previous night.

Remember your day can be fruitfully utilised if planned on the previous night. A time-bound action plan can ensure effective utilisation of the day. The same can assure you the achievement of a monthly plan, quarterly plan, six monthly plan and yearly plan.

Your planned day-to-day working only can assure you the achievement of the goals set by you within the time-bound frame. Also you will find that your lifetime goal can be achieved, and there is nothing that can stop you from **reaching the top.**

□

Exhaustive long brainstorming sessions in a boardroom meeting do not necessarily always churn out big ideas. Sometimes big ideas come from a low level.

Don't Overlook Great Ideas

In those days I was working as an 'Area Manager' with a leading company in the 'Fan Industry'. The company launched a new model of ceiling fan. The model was 'unique' in all respects. It was not comparable with any other fan in the country. Its unique design, aesthetic looks and technical superiority were unmatched. In order to ensure longer life of the fan motor, the company had enriched the fan with a 16-pole motor, as against 14-pole motor fans available in the market. On account of its design of 16-pole motor the fan had a stronger motor, which contained more silicon sheets and more enamelled copper wire. The motor as such was more powerful, and was designed to ensure a longer life.

But because of a greater number of poles it ran at a low RPM, which was by design and not by fault. Though the fan had a low speed (RPM), its air delivery was not poor. Increased blade angle had compensated the same.

Other popular models available in the market ran with a greater speed, but had a shorter life because of their 14-pole motors. Now because of their design they contained a lesser quantity of copper wire and a comparatively smaller

Accept good suggestions wherever they come from

armature (i.e. stator). It was therefore natural that they came cheaper. The customer had to pay less for those fans.

When this new model was launched, the company had great expectations from it. But when the customer had to pay nearly Rs. 400 more, he expected the fan to run at a greater speed without knowing that despite running at a low speed it delivered more air, and that it was technically far more superior than most of the fans available in the market.

It is a typical customer psychology. When he pays more, he expects a higher speed. It was not possible for the company to go to every customer and explain how this model was superior. The result was obvious. Most of the customers, who bought the fan, returned complaining of a low speed, without knowing that it was by design and not by fault. The dealers also did not take pains to explain the features to the customers. In most of the cases they themselves were ignorant about the features.

The result was that stocks began piling up with the dealers, and very soon the whole trade started talking about the failure of the model. Company's great expectations from it proved wrong.

When the model was being launched, I (as an 'Area Manager') had given a humble suggestion that since the customer chose a fan with a higher speed, the new model be launched with a 14-pole motor. **But the 'Top Management' ignored the suggestion, as it came from a comparatively low level.**

When the market response was found far below the

expectations, the top management called an urgent meeting. This showed the seriousness of the matter and the concern of the management. Again at this forum I repeated my suggestion, but it was turned down, as **the 'platform' from where I spoke was too low to be taken seriously.** No measurable step therefore could be taken, and the entire focus of the discussions remained around matters like pricing, discounts, schemes and other issues relating to the skills of the sales force. The purpose of conducting the meeting stood defeated.

It was only natural that the response in the market place remained unaltered. *My years of experience and a better product knowledge compared to most seniors, coupled with the in-depth study of customer psychology, and the pulse of the market had enriched me to be able to express my views.* I was feeling restless, as I knew what the real cause of the problem was. But I was feeling helpless, as the platform, where I stood was too low to be taken seriously.

The following month the CMD of the company paid a visit to our branch. The same matter again surfaced during the discussions in the meeting that was conducted to review the branch working.

This time, I again grabbed the opportunity to express my views. **But the platform, which was already low for the top management, seemed still lower from the height of the CMD's level**. The CMD pleaded that if the fan was given with a 14-pole motor, it would lose its technical superiority.

The result was only natural. The model could not

generate demand in the market. Finally, after experiencing more than two years of lukewarm response, the design of the model was changed. This time the fan was given with a 14-pole motor. **This was exactly what I had been suggesting. But this time the decision was taken because the suggestion came from the top**. But till then it was too late, and a period of two years was enough to cause damage.

Actually this is a universal problem. It is quite unfortunate for us that we live in a society, where **"who is saying it carries more importance, rather than what he or she is saying".**

As a result thousands of great ideas die every day without being noticed and acted on.

"Exhaustive long brainstorming sessions in a boardroom meeting do not necessarily always churn out big ideas. Sometimes big ideas come from a low level".

I remember how an ordinary mechanic in our company designed a bearing-puller. A very effective and low cost bearing-puller that was far more superior to the pullers available at a very high price in the market.

You will notice that often very effective suggestions come from a low level. They can really pay dividends, if taken seriously and acted on.

Make it a point. Don't overlook a great idea, even if it comes from a low level. Sometimes great ideas come from a low level. You are deprived of the dividends if you overlook them. □

What you say is important,
but how you say is
more important.

Communicate Effectively

Have you ever thought why one would listen to a person carefully and attentively, while he refuses to listen to another person? Why is it that students wait for a particular professor's period, while they try to skip another professor's period? Why do we find a person interesting while he talks to us, but find another person boring?

Often people mix-up an effective communication with big vocabulary. But it is not true. Look around you at those, whom you consider effective communicators, and you will find that they do not necessarily have big vocabulary. In fact you will find that many of them do not have a formal education. But they are effective communicators. Not because they use great sounding words, but because they know well, whom they are talking to. They know which language they will understand, and above all they know what to say and how to say. One thing is common in all effective communicators. "They have something to say and they have a burning desire for others to hear to what they say".

Remember: "What you say is important, but how you say is more important".

While graduating, one professor, who taught us mathematics, once made a very impressive statement. He said, he would consider himself a good teacher, only if no student failed in the subject he taught. And he really had that history. No student ever failed in his subject. In fact many students, who considered mathematics, a boring and absolutely dry subject, found it interesting only after they attended his lectures.

This professor always kept in mind the problems of an average student. He knew well, which language an average student would understand. He did not believe in great sounding words. That was why he used language that average students understood. He would often make a proper mix of other live subjects, or some light jokes and his subject, to keep the entire classroom alive. His lectures were never boring. Students never thought of skipping his lectures. They in fact waited for him.

In the middle of the session he was transferred to another college. The news spread and students got worried.

The new professor was altogether different. He, unlike his predecessor, never cared for the students. He would simply start his lectures, and would jump from one example to another; and from one chapter to the next, without caring whether the students understood, what he taught. He made the subject so dull and boring, that the students saw no loss in skipping his lectures. Also students were often seen napping in his periods. He would often use fillers like "Hey you, what are you doing there?" Or "I warn you to be attentive", but the students were not interested to listen to what he said, because he himself was not interested. It seemed as if he himself had no interest in the subject, he taught. Also he never seemed to have owned the students. The result was only natural. He got the response he deserved.

To make your lecture or presentation effective, the first condition is "own your audience". This is because fear of the unknown is a natural phenomenon. If members of your audience are sure, you are one of them, and that they are going to be benefited from what you are going to say, they will accept you. The second important point is, never try to use high sounding words unnecessarily. You will find that all successful orators use simple language.

It has been seen that almost all the successful orators invariably keep checking whether their audience are with them. Make it a habit. It will help you a lot. **Check, whether you are getting the response from your audience that you are expecting.** If yes, proceed further. If not, you probably need to make some changes.

Develop a habit of crosschecking: Do you remember how more than 300 passengers lost their lives in an aeroplane accident a few years ago near Delhi? A few days after the accident, a probe was ordered into the accident. The findings revealed that the main cause was only a communication gap.

According to the reports, the Air Traffic Control asked

the pilot of an aircraft (sailing at an altitude of 18,000 feet) to come down to 15,000 feet, to maintain a safe distance from another aircraft sailing at the same altitude. But the Russian pilot possibly did not understand the instructions given by the ATC, and maintained the same altitude. As a result the two aircraft collided amid the air, and more than 300 passengers met a gruesome end. Now in this case, the accident could have been avoided, had the ATC crosschecked whether the instructions given by them were fully understood by the Russian pilot.

The above accident proves how precarious a communication gap may be. Though it may not always be precarious, but if not removed, it may lead to a situation, where the purpose of communicating stands defeated. Always make sure, your audience are with you, and your message is going to them without changing its shape.

The art of conversation

Why don't they listen: Most of us are more fond of talking than listening to others. Therefore during your presentation or conversation, if you get a feeling that your audience is not listening to you, you are probably right. Your audience's mind may have wandered.

Several factors contribute to this. Knowing these factors will help to overcome them.

How bad is our listening

- We use only one-fourth of our listening capacity.

- We use only one-tenth of our memory potential.
- We distort what little we remember.

Reasons for bad listening

- We have a very short attention span.
- We are not taught listening, like we are taught reading or writing.
- We filter what others say through all kinds of screens.
- Our thinking speed is 4 times our hearing speed.

Our average minimum thinking speed is about 400 words per minute.

Our average speaking/hearing speed is about 125 words per minute.

Therefore the listener's mind is free for 275 words per minute.

We don't listen to those we consider

1. Inferior.
2. Not very credible.
3. Unattractive.

To ensure good listening take care of the following:

1. Ensure your audience are comfortable. Pay heed to the environment.
2. Check for use of jargon, droop, stringing or staccato.
3. Change volume modulation, speed and use silence (short or long pauses).
4. Use visuals, cartoons/ sketches/ photographs, etc.

to maintain the interest of your audience.

5. Make use of your body movements and facial expressions.

Note: Point No. 2 in the above list asks to check use of droop, stringing and staccato.

Drooping is associated with dropping final consonants. (Example: - just – jus, going –goin, thousand – thousan, etc.).

Stringing is associated with speaking too fast, whereas staccato means speaking in bursts, or bouncing words unevenly.

How to make an oral presentation effective

While preparing yourself for an oral presentation, remember that your audience is a gathering of human beings like you, and therefore they may have the same likes, dislikes, fears and interests like you. The following points will help you prepare for an effective oral presentation:

1. Remember that the human mind is comfortable with its present state of thinking. It starts feeling uncomfortable at the idea of changing this state.
2. Fear of the unknown is a normal human phenomenon. The audience does not know what the speaker is about to say. The survival instinct of the audience, perceives the speaker as a threat. A threat to the survival of the audience's present way of thinking.

Therefore when a speaker comes before it, the audience

would first like to assess the extent of the perceived threat. Only then will it open its mind to the speaker's thoughts.

The first 90 seconds are very important, as in these 90 seconds your audience assess you, and treat you accordingly. These 90 seconds consist of 3 Vs.

1. First 30 seconds (Visual content).
2. Next 30 seconds (Vocal content).
3. Next 30 seconds (Verbal content).

What the speaker's words mean to them.

Visual content: Before starting your presentation or speech ask yourself, "How do I look, appear and behave"? Do I look aggressive and intimidating? Or Do I look meek and unsure? Or Do I look friendly and confident?

Effective use of the body can add impact to the presentation. Approach the stage calmly and unhurriedly. Greet the audience with an honest pleasant smile. Look at the entire group rather than only one side of the room. Maintain relaxed, pleasant and conversational expressions. Avoid strong deadpan look.

Vocal content: Speak slow enough to be understood. But fast enough to maintain energy.

Use pauses:

1. Before or after a key term.
2. To separate items in a series.
3. To indicate a major break in your thoughts.

Avoid speaking too slow, which may be boring.

Verbal content: This is probably the most important content of a speech, as it is associated with what the speaker's words mean to the audience. Therefore it must be planned smartly. To plan it effectively and smartly, ask yourself these questions:

- When am I speaking?
- Where am I speaking?
- Who am I speaking to?
- Why am I speaking?
- What should I speak?
- How should I speak?

Edit the length and time before the presentation. Remember that an ideal speech or presentation is long enough, so that the subject is fully covered, but short enough, so that the interest of the audience is maintained. Edit flow and continuity. Prepare for most likely questions. Prepare the answers for those likely questions. Use simple and short sentences. Avoid use of complicated and long sentences. You may use small cards containing the main points. Arrange these cards to maintain the correct order and flow. The use of these cards however must be done smartly. There is no need to hide them from your audience. Keep these cards on the podium or table, and keep turning them as you go along from one point to the next.

Remove any negative thoughts about the audience. Remove any feeling that they are against you.

The most important factor, which decides the impact of your presentation, is possibly hidden in, how you start and how you end. Remember that the audience's memory is very strong for what you say in the beginning and what you say while concluding. Following figure will show you the audience's memory curve.

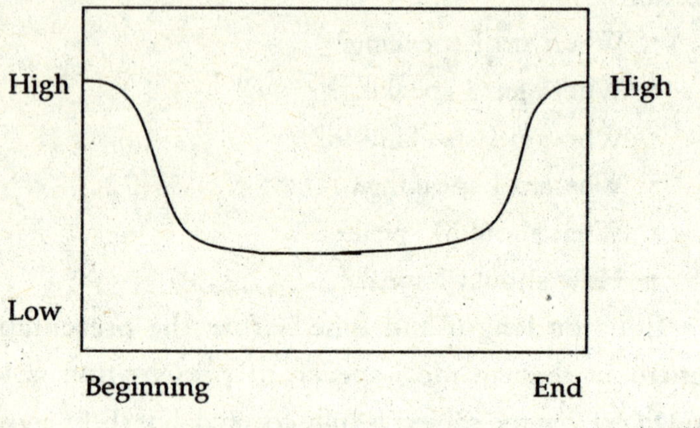

□

Think Creatively

Look at the beautiful world around you. Have a look at the amazing instruments that you use. Look at the astonishing inventions, which are the outcome of creative thinking. Think a little about how life saving drugs must have been formulated, and you will know how creative thinking can do miracles.

Those highly successful people, who have achieved something big, do not necessarily have extraordinary intellect. Their creative thinking has possibly played an important role in their success.

It is only creative thinking, which paves your way to larger success. And don't worry. Creative thinking is not reserved for a particular class or a particular income bracket. Anyone has a right to think creatively.

Wherever you are, and whatever you do, ask yourself "how can I do it better?" If you ask yourself, "can I do it better?", the chances are very bleak for you to do it in a better way. This thought possibly is not likely to show you the way to do things differently. Instead, ask yourself, "how can I do it better?", and you will find yourself actively involved in thinking for better ways to do it. This question will put your mind in motion, and will show you the way to do it better.

Without creative thinking we would not have been able to watch a cricket match on a TV set, sitting in our drawing room, once restricted to those, sitting in the stadium. The invention of a television is a result of creative thinking.

Without creative thinking, we wouldn't have been able to fly in the sky in an aeroplane, once considered a reserved province for the birds.

Creative thinking helps you everywhere. Use every minute that you get, in creative thinking. You don't need big qualifications to think creatively.

How does creative thinking help?

My counterpart heading a department in a corporate house had an opening for a 'Sales Officer'. He floated an ad. in a local daily. Many applications poured in. After scrutiny he called a few for an interview.

He was highly impressed with a particular guy who had a 'tremendous' memory. He could produce any data instantly without straining his brain. He remembered the important dates of history. He could tell the exact date when our national heroes were born. In fact he displayed the efficiency of his brain like a computer.

When my friend sought my opinion, I showed my reluctance pleading that one has to think creatively to improve the business. I also wondered how possibly my friend could use the data stored in his brain, without creative thinking.

I don't really know what prompted my friend to opt for his services. But the truth is that he chose to give this man the letter of intent.

But the kind of job he was in, needed creative thinking and planned work. The history stored in his brain had nothing to do with his business. This guy didn't think creatively. It was only expected that he could produce no results. Also he found that he wasn't meant for this kind of job, so naturally he was feeling uncomfortable. As the pressure mounted, he became more inadequate, and finally when he realised, he was at the wrong place, he had no options left for him, but to move out.

Remember: It is not important how much knowledge you have. What is important is how creatively you use your knowledge.

It is not how much you know, that counts. It is how you use, what you know, that counts. It is great to remember the history and make your brain a data bank. But it is of no use, if you can't use it creatively.

For reproducing the data any one can buy a computer. Why will a company pay a fat salary to a person who has made his brain a 'warehouse' of history and facts and figures, when the same can be done with a machine?

I often tell people that creative thinking is not restricted to a particular class, and neither does it need a certain qualification.

Your brain is an amazing instrument. A human being is a rare species, who has been given this amazing instrument by nature. Don't make it a warehouse of facts and figures of history. Use it for creative thinking. Data stored in it has no value, unless put to use.

I have seen job seekers trying to create sympathy for them by telling the employers how badly they need the employment. Once I interviewed a guy, who touched my feet after showing me the picture of his poverty, his two younger brothers and an old sick mother, who wholly depended on him.

By telling such stories one can gain sympathy, but cannot get a job. In today's competitive environment no one has time to listen to the stories. Corporate houses are not there for charity. They mean business. They can run the show only if they make profits. And to make profits they need people, who can bring new ideas in. They need those, who are competent and who promise progress.

Gaining sympathy doesn't help any one. Such sympathy comes at the cost of self-respect. Emphasise instead, on your qualities. One doesn't have to implore for a job, if he proves his worth. In fact there is a short supply of creative thinkers. And therefore, there is less competition among those who think creatively.

Use time in creative thinking. See how you can do things in a better way. Perfection is something non-existent. There is always scope for improvement. And betterment needs creativity. Think creatively and see miracles happen. □

Be an Effective Leader

A leader is a person who leads. I believe that an ideal leader is like 'a thumb' in a palm. And you know the importance of the thumb. Imagine how difficult it will be to lift articles without the help of your thumb. Be it a small glass of water or a book, you can't lift it without the help of your thumb. Try to scribble a few lines on a piece of paper without using your thumb, and you will realise its importance. It is quite amazing to see that the thumb doesn't lift any article by itself, but it helps the other fingers lift articles. An ideal leader is just like a thumb. He makes his team members work. He works as a catalyst for them. He guides them.

It is said that **"a team of sheep led by a lion can beat a team of lions led by a sheep."** That is the importance of a leader in a team. An efficient and effective leader stands head above the shoulder. He takes his team to new heights. An inefficient leader not only reduces the performance to shambles, but also destroys the spirits of his team members.

An ideal leader is like the thumb in your palm

When you assume the responsibility of a group as its leader, you are expected to ensure that the members of your team perform well. As a boss you not only have to make them work, but also have to make sure, they grow. Ensure that they feel secure under your wings and can dream progress. Being a leader your role demands much more from you. Have a look at some of the most important qualities of an effective leader.

Never condemn your predecessor

It is seen that in order to build their own image fast, some managers are induced to condemn their predecessors. While doing so, they tend to forget that the person, whom they are condemning, has worked in close contact with all the other members for a pretty long period, and as such must have certainly developed a liking for him among the team members. By criticising him they not only display their immaturity, but also raise a question mark about their own integrity.

Mr. Smith was sent to a branch as a manager, where things were not really in shape. The sales were at their lowest levels, in line with the morale of the branch people. When he took over charge of the branch, pending claims looked like mountains of promises, which were not kept. Collections hardly came in time. Things were in a really bad shape. The result was that the team members felt insecure. Smith had a tough task ahead of him. On one side, he had to ensure that the business started improving smoothly, on the other side, he had to make sure that his teammates didn't feel insecure. He took many decisions to make the workplace a point of attraction, where people enjoyed working. He activated the staff club and conducted the family get-togethers periodically. These get-togethers brought people closer to each other and developed belongingness in them for the office. People started loving the office atmosphere, as it gave them and their family members a booster dose, necessary to perform better. Earlier it looked like a tiger's den. And the reason was simple. People knew the branch was not performing. And since the branch was not performing, everybody in the branch felt insecure.

Smith gave them the confidence that they had all the capabilities in them, and that they could turn the table round. He empowered them and started giving them responsibilities. Soon the picture began to change. Within months the same branch started delivering results. Smith worked for close to five years in the same branch. In those five years the branch touched new heights. The trade started looking at the branch and branch people with respect. It was natural that Smith also was looked at with respect. The respect he deserved.

The top management realised his importance, and he was sent to a larger branch. This gesture of the top management towards Smith was clearly a sign of recognition and approval of his style of working.

The person, who took over his charge, had a totally different working style. Let me call this new manager Mr.

Frank. Immediately after taking over charge from Smith, Frank called a meeting of all the team members. It was a good gesture and the team members thought probably Mr. Frank would extend a vote of thanks, and would express his gratitude to Smith, who had run the show so successfully for nearly five years.

But each one was taken aback when Mr. Frank disapproved of everything happening in the branch till now. His remarks were something like "whatever was happening in the branch till yesterday was wrong, and the real work will begin today". His remarks clearly showed he liked nothing of his predecessor. He carried an impression as if nothing good happened to the branch in the last five years. His first ever address as the branch head to the team members looked like an attempt to prove that the branch had witnessed nothing positive in Smith's tenure.

While condemning his predecessor, Mr. Frank overlooked the fact, that the top management had shown confidence in him, by giving him a larger responsibility. Had he been an ineffective leader, he would not have delivered results. Even if Mr. Frank felt certain changes necessary, he shouldn't have forgotten that all the team members respected Smith, and as such they wouldn't like his criticism, especially by a newcomer who had still to prove himself.

Mr. Frank didn't try to go into the depth, and started introducing changes. He didn't find it necessary to study why Smith took certain decisions in a different manner. It appeared as if he was sent to the branch, only to undo all that Smith did. He saw everything wrong and nothing right.

It was felt that Mr. Frank would ensure, he did something differently, whether right or wrong. The result was only expected. The branch that had begun giving results, again started its downward journey. The sales started sliding. Within the period of a year and a half, the branch once again was in a shambles. When Mr. Frank left the branch, it ranked the last among the contenders.

Mark it well. Effective leaders never condemn their predecessors. No one ever won respect of the team members by condemning his predecessor. Even if you want to make certain changes, don't ever try to criticise your predecessor. Show full respect for him. Don't ever forget, whatever he did, must have been the need of the hour. Probably you would have taken the same decisions too, had you been in his place. Visualise, how you would like to be remembered by your successor. Would you like to be remembered by your successor, the way you remember your predecessor? Ask yourself this question. The answer will show you the proper way.

Take people along

When a new manager takes charge of a set-up, it is natural and only expected that he is full of energy. He is enthusiastic, and wants to introduce many changes. And he is surely not wrong if he wants to introduce certain systems, or wants to make certain changes. In many cases he has to. Else he will not be able to extract the best out of his co-workers. **"Also sometimes a change is required to break the monotony."** Changes pump in new breath in the system. You see, how a person working in the same chair and doing the same routine job, over a period of several years loses his interest. This affects his productivity. Sometimes changes are necessary to fill new enthusiasm.

Sometimes when a new leader takes charge of a set-up, he is expected to bring in many changes. But it is easier said than done. **"Firstly and most importantly, a human mind is the most change-resistant thing known in the world."** Secondly, prolonged working in a particular fashion, over a period gives birth to lethargy and complacency. The result is you have a bunch of people who have lost their edge. When a new leader comes in, he is nothing less than an enigma. People look at him with anxiety. While they carefully watch every activity that he does, they also try to adjust themselves with him.

Sometimes they are not prepared to welcome the new changes imposed on them. This is not a result of unwillingness to work. The simple reason is they are not taken into confidence. **"The result is they take new changes as a hurricane, which will grab their peace of mind."**

If you take charge of a group, mark it well. To get your team members to accept the changes that you want to bring in, you must involve them. Make them a party. Let them know why certain changes are being brought in. **"The best way to make them accept the changes is, let the**

changes be suggested by them." Let it be their decision. After you have completed the introductory formalities, and find that the dust has settled, call a meeting. Put the major problems that need an immediate intervention before them. Allow your teammates to scratch their heads. *"There is every chance that the changes that you want to introduce, will be suggested by them."*

The biggest advantage of carrying out this exercise will be that, now the changes are not forcefully imposed upon them. As your teammates have opted for them, they own them. **"Now they see what you want them to see."** You now find that your goal has become their goal. "You are not running on different tracks." You now find that you have made matters a lot simpler than ever before.

Mark it well: You make things a lot easier when you involve the entire team. Don't go alone. Let all the team members go along.

Stand by their side

When you are the leader of a group, your role changes a lot. You are not only the boss; you also have to play the role of a mentor. As a leader you have to ensure that your subordinates grow. It gives you great satisfaction to see your subordinates grow. Don't forget that your own growth is a result of their hard work and their growth will further push you up.

It is quite likely that when one works, he is likely to make many mistakes. You don't get tailor-made people. "No one is all good or all bad." Each one has some pluses and some minuses. As a boss your role is to extract the best out of them. I have seen managers who don't lose an opportunity to pinpoint the mistakes committed by their subordinates. Such practice never brings any positive results. Their fault-finding nature stops their co-workers from doing anything creative. Remember; they are willing to work, and can do miracles. Give them a free hand. Show faith in them. Make them feel, you need them. Make them feel important.

When anything goes wrong, panic hangs around. This is because a probe is initiated. This is the time when they need you the most. Sometimes mistakes happen unknowingly. They are not always the outcome of wrong intentions. When you find your team member has done something wrong unintentionally, you must stand by him. Assure your seniors that this was only a mistake, and in future the same will not be repeated. At the same time ensure at your level that the same mistake doesn't occur again. Don't reprimand your team members for mistakes. Give them the necessary guidance. They must find you standing by their side when they are in trouble.

Remember; you can win the faith of your team members only when they feel safe under your wings.

Practise appreciation: When your subordinates do something new, they expect a word of appreciation from you. A word of recognition gives them confidence. It gives them the tonic necessary to perform their work more effectively. Appreciate even their small accomplishments.

It doesn't cost you anything. But what you get in return is of a great value. If you see a colleague comes to the workplace neatly and perfectly dressed, tell him that you like his dress choice. Make him feel, you take notice when he does something better. Compliment your teammates for their children's achievements. Try to attend their important family functions like marriages of their children. This will bring them closer to you.

When you find, a person has done exceedingly well in a specific task, ask him to share his experience with others. While it will motivate him, others will be inspired too.

I remember an annual meet of a company, in which New Year budgets were to be discussed and finalised. Before finalising the New Year budgets, the previous year's results were announced. The best three performers were identified from the lot who had given maximum growth. The first person who headed a division had joined the company only three months back, and hence was actually not responsible for the performance of his division, but was asked to make a presentation, as now he headed the division.

He rose and started speaking. He narrated how things were in a mess when he took over. He said, "When I came nothing was in shape." "Everything", he continued, "was in bad shape, people ran directionless. This was the time, I realised how difficult was my task. But I was committed. I started taking action. I struggled a lot. I did this, and I did that...", he continued.

As he went along, I could clearly see the resentment

growing on the faces of his sales force. As this manager had joined only three months ago, he had hardly done anything. His division's success was a result of the hard work of his salesmen. But for his personal glory their hard work was completely being ignored. They felt betrayed.

Now actually speaking, this fellow had got a great opportunity to win over the faith of his team. He could have used this opportunity to motivate his sales force. But instead, he squandered it for his personal glory. While doing that, he completely neglected their hard work. Not only this, he also forgot that the Vice-President was not a fool. He was sharp enough to understand, what kind of a leader this person would make.

After his presentation was complete, the second person was called who headed another division. This person had a different approach altogether. The first thing he said was "I am extremely thankful to the management for giving me this honour," but, what my division has done, was a result of the hard work of my team members. Then he asked each member of his sales force to come over to the dais, and complimented each one of them individually. He then said, "I'm very sure I will get the same support from all of you the next year and in the years to come". He clearly was a winner, as by sharing his success with his salesmen he motivated them and won their support.

While in the first case, the leader failed to motivate his team members, in the second case the leader used the opportunity fully to motivate his team, and had made sure, his team members performed still better the next year.

Remember: A sincere appreciation doesn't cost you anything. But what you get in return is of a great value. "Invest appreciation and win the support of your team."

Treat people with respect: Have you noticed how each person in this world is different from another? Each person has a different face, different voice, different nose, different understanding. In fact no two persons are identical. Each one has different likes and dislikes. You name the quality, and you find that no two persons will make the same combination. Even in the case of twins, you will find that except for the face, both the individuals differ from each other in every aspect. Yes this is truth. **"Each single person in this world is unique of his kind."** And hence deserves respect.

Mark it well. Every single human being in this world wants to be treated with respect. No one has ever won friends by taking others for granted. Big bosses who, sitting in their ivory towers think that people reporting to them are doing nothing more than their duty, and therefore don't need to be treated with respect, are always on the wrong track. They never win respect. **Dictators don't last long.** They realise their mistake only when they step down, but then it is too late to realise, and hence of no use.

When you pass on instructions to your subordinates, think twice on your way of giving them instructions. Visualise, would you like to receive orders from your boss, the way you order them? Would you like the language to be used for you, that you use for them? I have seen managers becoming very harsh while talking to their subordinates. This is possibly because they carry a feeling, that best results can be taken only by tightening them.

In some cases it is because of the **'paranoia'** about their subordinates. "This **paranoid fear** is seen in case, especially when the boss has a doubt about his own capability", and knows that his subordinate is more efficient or more knowledgeable. In such cases the bosses have been found fearful or insecure about their subordinates. **A boss, nourishing fear that his subordinate can overtake him, is a dangerous situation.**

This is a hazardous situation. In such cases everybody and every side tend to be the loser. The boss, who is always under pressure, is almost always busy in finding ways to prove where his subordinate went wrong. The subordinate is a loser because his boss doesn't miss a single opportunity to let him down. The outcome is a big zero. Such a situation is most 'unhealthy' situation for any organisation.

As a group leader, if you have an outstanding talent in your team, don't ever try to suppress him. Never try to hold him back. Make the best use of his talent. Give him more opportunities. Try to give him more exposure. Avoid paranoid fears. Don't worry if you find that he is outstanding. Organisations take extra care of such people. He can prove an indispensable person and an important asset for you and for the organisation as well.

To make the best use of such people, give them

additional responsibilities. See how they can be useful for their other colleagues who need to improve. Make them feel important. Let such people outshine. Don't try to scratch off the natural glow of a diamond. Don't misbehave with them for your personal gains.

Don't ever forget. You have a set of people, some more efficient, others a little less. You have a reason to treat them differently. But treat them with respect. Avoid any paranoid fear. It will not take you anywhere.

Develop an affection for people: There can be various reasons for you to like or dislike a particular person. In fact every single human being has certain likes and dislikes. You like or dislike a person because of some of his habits. And every single person has a right to do that. I cannot enlighten about the gains of disliking a person, but I surely know the advantages of liking him. Have you ever tried to know the opinion of a person about you, whom you dislike? What do you think he should say about you? Obviously the same. The chances are not more than one in a thousand, that he will say something good about you. The reason is simple. **"You reap what you sow."**

Next time when you find, that you dislike a person for any reason, try to exercise this. Make up your mind and tell yourself that you have to like him. Make a list of his assets. But be honest to yourself. Make sure, your effort has to be sincere. Try to look at his good habits. Go a little deep and have a look at the reasons for liking him, and you will find many. "You will find that there are more reasons to like him than to dislike." When you develop liking for a person, you find that he likes you too. Just opposite to it, when you hate a person, you can't expect him to like you.

Peter Hocks was a good guitarist. He was a well-known figure in the music circles. Often he had stolen the show away in programmes by displaying the magic of his fingers on the strings of his guitar. He had many friends and well-wishers. But for reasons better known to him he always hated to talk to Rodricks who played jazz. Both moved in the same friends circle. But no one knew the reason why Peter Hocks hated Rodricks. Years went past. They shared the same friends, but never shared the thoughts with each other.

It was only a music concert that changed Peter's attitude towards Rodricks. After a few performances, Peter appeared on the stage. He literally stole the show away. There was a big round of applause after his performance. Like any other artiste, Peter also loved the audience's response, and like any other person, wanted others in his circle to know, how he was appreciated.

It was a real pleasant surprise for him the next day when his friends greeted him for his excellent performance on the previous night, and told him how Rodricks was all praise for him. They also told him how Rodricks always praised his command on the strings of the guitar. Now it was Peter's turn to react. He was forced to deem, whether there was any reason at all to dislike Rodricks. He was forced to think, "Why a person, whom I hate, should have all praise for me?" And that very day he changed his opinion about Rodricks.

Know it well. No one has ever won friends by disliking people. No one is perfect. This is a universal truth. **"Perfection is something non-existent."** It exists only in your imagination. You have to accept people as they are. Don't be mistaken. Others will like you only if you like them.

Use positive language

There are many factors that play an important role in the success of a team. Team-spirit and motivation level have a greater significance. Every team leader wants his team to be fully motivated. But in most cases the 'big bosses' choose the wrong way to do so. While they believe, they are motivating the team, they are in fact 'unknowingly' destroying the motivation level. It may sound absurd, but it is true. The reason is simple. In most cases the big bosses tend to believe that it is always threatening language that works. But in fact it is the other way round.

As a team leader you have different ways to pass on your message to your team members. Two different sentences *"the glass is half filled"* and *"the glass is half empty"* reveal the same meaning, yet project two different pictures. Similarly you may pass on a message to your team in many ways.

When you have to pass on a message to your team members, remember that while talking to them you project a picture. Every sentence uttered by you creates an image in their minds. A person does not think in figures or graphs. He or she thinks in images and pictures. A human mind is an amazing instrument. As soon as it perceives a sound, it automatically gets activated in creating the pictures relating to it. When you say something, you in fact project pictures. By this token we can say that a human being is a projector.

When you say, *"I'm sorry to inform you that our mission has miserably failed"*, people see only a defeat. But if the same thing is said in words like *"I have got a bright idea, which I'm sure, will give us great success", people* see a great achievement waiting for them. If you say *"you've got to do it, whether you like it or not, or be prepared for the consequences"*, people see something unpleasant to do. But if you say the same thing in words like, *"pull up your socks friends", we cannot afford to lose an opportunity like this"*, people get enthusiastic, as they see victory standing in front of them.

As a leader you have to ensure an excellent performance from your team members. Promise them victory and win support. Show them the path that encourages them for greater accomplishments. No one can expect wonders by creating panic. Avoid using negative sounding words. **Use positive language.**

Don't expect from them what you can't do

It is frequently seen that the bosses show great expectations from the team members, which are far from the 'ground reality'. A group leader must know what is possible and what is not. Before expecting from your subordinates anything, ask yourself with full honesty, *can I do it myself what I'm expecting them to do?*

Can you imagine a teacher asking the students a question that he himself cannot answer? Years ago I have worked in close contact with a friend, who headed a division. He had a unique working style. He believed that he could take results by merely citing the figures and ordering the subordinates to achieve them. When he had only two months of the financial year left for him, and a great task ahead, he thought, it was high time he pulled the strings to ensure a great closing. The way he chose was really amazing. He took out a notepad, and scribbled the figures, he had in mind. These figures contained the targets for the next two months, and the proposed new dealers' appointments. The figures drawn were glamorous, but anyone who knew the markets well, could easily say, they were impossible to be achieved. During the meeting he said everything that he felt was necessary, but failed to guide them about how to proceed.

The boys went into the markets and slogged for a fortnight, only to return empty-handed. With their faces hung, when they sought his help, he burst out on them and planned his visits to all the areas one-by-one. He really pushed himself hard, which was a commendable gesture, but when faced the ground realities of the markets, he realised that what he expected, was something impossible. One can easily imagine the kind of situation it would make, if a boss reprimands his subordinates for falling short in achieving a given task, but utterly fails when he tries himself.

Be sure, you expect from your team members only what is possible. Merely telling them to do something, which you know well, is impossible, may snatch their enthusiasm and discourage them. Further, in case of failures, you should be able to guide them. Throw yourself into the assignment, and show them how it can be done. Only then can you command their respect.

Don't form opinions fast

Sometimes people tend to form fast opinions about things. They do so to arrest the situation quickly. But hurried actions do not always necessarily help you. Develop the habit of going into the depth, and study the reasons why certain things are, the way they are. Try to go a little deep, and spend some time in studying, why certain decisions were taken in a particular fashion. There are all chances that you will have to rethink.

Mr. Michael was otherwise a very sharp person who learnt things quickly, but had a bad habit of forming opinions fast. He often had to change his decisions later when he realised, he was wrong. But such occasions would create embarrassing situations for him. And the reason was simple. Most of his decisions were based on the quick opinion he formed in his mind about things.

When he paid his first 'introductory' visit to all important clients, he didn't find it necessary to spend some time in the office to know the history of those, he was scheduled to visit. He, in his journey cycle visited a client, who had been discontinued by the company for his late payments and misconduct with many senior officials. To add to it, he often deducted huge amounts from his payments against many imaginary claims, which never existed. He was given numerous chances to change, but all in vain.

When Michael visited him, he gave Michael the treatment, only VIPs are given. He did everything that was necessary to impress Michael. It was not out of his love for Michael. It was his business interest, which forced him to project a different image of himself. Michael was highly impressed with his magnificent and glamorous edifice. This client not only projected big pictures before Michael, but also showed his willingness to restart business if he was given a chance.

Michael immediately contacted the office, and wanted to know, why this party was discontinued. It was only expected that he reinstated the party. Initially things looked quite smooth. But soon the party again started to behave, the way he was known for. In the coming months Michael was left with no options, but to stop supplies to him. This time it proved expensive, as the company had to collect a huge amount from him, and the party had stopped making payments.

Sometimes you are lured to form your opinion fast, because you tend to believe, the things are exactly, the way they appear. But in most cases they are not. Even if they are, it is not necessary to make your opinion public. It is better to keep your opinion close to your chest. Watch for some days. Possibly you may think differently the next month. This is applicable in all the situations. Allow the dust to settle.

I have seen numerous cases, in which the innocent were penalised for a lifetime, only because somebody formed a quick opinion about them. The very first glimpse does not necessarily give you the correct picture of a situation or a person. Try to control your emotions before taking actions based on quick opinions. Time is the best remedy to avoid mistakes of this nature. Only what is required is your patience.

Be an ideal example for them

Have you ever tried to study the actions of a person? Have you tried to study whom he acts like? While at home, at the workplace, or may be in a public place, next time try to go a little deep and you will find it interesting too. You will find that almost every act of a person is influenced by someone. And this someone is none other than the one he finds **'Mr. Ideal.'**

You will often find students, imitating their ideal teacher. At home you will find children, acting like their parents. It not only gives them satisfaction, but also at the same time they unknowingly try to imbibe the qualities of those, they find ideal. The way a person walks, the way he eats or drinks. The way he speaks, pauses or even his selection of words, almost everything is influenced by somebody. These comparatively unimportant small habits reveal, what sort of environment he lives in. This however is one side of the coin, which projects only the natural habits of a person to imitate certain habits of another person. What is more important is the other side of the coin, which points to the person being copied.

When a person takes charge of a group as its leader, there are many things that happen to him. While people take notice of whatever he does, they at the same time also try to adapt themselves to him, and in doing so, over a period they unknowingly imbibe many of his habits. In many cases I have seen that subordinates have picked up many qualities from their bosses. In fact it is natural too. They are seen copying their bosses through relatively small and unimportant actions.

If you have taken over the charge of a group as its leader, remember, you are a source of inspiration for others. Every action of yours is being watched carefully by the whole group. *"Therefore it is important for you to behave the way, you expect them to behave."* You naturally can't expect them to come to the office on time if you are a regular latecomer. If you want them to take the work seriously, you will have to doubly make sure, your own approach towards it is not casual. If you have a habit to leave your work in the middle just because the office hours are over, you naturally can't expect your subordinates to stay back till they complete it.

Make sure, you go to the workplace neatly dressed. Only then you can expect others to maintain their dress standard. How can you expect others to be honest to their job, if you have a habit to manipulate your tour expense statements? To get them to be enthusiastic, you must be enthusiastic first.

Years ago when I was a Sales Manager, I used to visit those small places where the public transport was very poor. In a particular case my subordinate was confronting a problem in a small town, which he could not solve despite several visits to the town. I wanted to arrest the situation immediately, and planned a visit to the town along with him.

It was a very hot day in the middle of peak summers. For certain reasons I wanted to avoid travelling by car or taking a private taxi, which could have given us great comfort. Also it was the need of the hour, which demanded for a cut on travelling expenses. We decided to take a bus. But it was very crowded, and my assistant was wondering how I could possibly travel in such conditions. We were both dripping wet with sweat. He possibly expected me to curse the odd conditions of public transport, or at least be irritated, but was surprised to see me smiling. He couldn't stop himself from asking me how I was feeling travelling in a crowded bus on such a hot day. He asked me, "you must be feeling uncomfortable, aren't you?" I smiled and said, "I certainly do." ***"But when I think of my family, and when I imagine that my wife and my child are enjoying the cool comfort at home, only because I am travelling like this, I just forget everything".*** This feeling relieves me from any negative thoughts caused by such uncomfortable travelling.

My answer had penetrated his emotions, and had touched the depths of his heart. He later on quoted this example to many others, and most importantly, never complained thereafter about painful working conditions, as he knew well, it was necessary for the comfort of his family. After all whom do you work for? ***If you are honest to those, you love, you will be honest to your job too.***

Mark it well. As a leader, you are a source of inspiration for others. They learn from you, and to learn they copy you. Be an ideal example for them. "Make sure they copy only the right things." **Ask yourself, "Am I worth being copied?"** Make sure the original is worth being copied.

□

Use the Manpower Smartly

In the initial years of my career, I used to visit a cooperative society run by a huge steel plant. The society bought lots of material from us regularly. As I paid frequent visits to this society, I developed close relations with many of its employees, Managers who headed various departments, and the president of the society. Sometimes we used to sit for hours, and discuss the in-house problems and other matters related to the working of the society. On one such occasion the president told me a very interesting case of a particular employee. This employee was a real problem for almost all the managers. No one wanted him in his department. Wherever he went, he remained a constant source of pain for his seniors and other co-workers. People avoided talking to him. Let me call this person 'Mr. Albert'.

People saw all negative points in him. He was not only reluctant to work by himself, but also created obstacles for others who wanted to work. He worked with many supervisors, many managers and with almost all the colleagues. But everyone carried more or less the same opinion about him. In everyone's estimation he was a person, who was good-for-nothing. His record was full of adverse remarks, which spoke nothing good about him. The result was, after a few months he would be shifted from one department to the other. But the outcome was the same. He remained a constant source of headache for others. When it became difficult for his seniors to accommodate him and use him anywhere, they sent his file to the president for action against him.

The president was a sharp person. He was an expert in human psychology. He studied the file a little deeper. He discovered some interesting facts. He found that each time when Albert was sent to a new department, only his working place changed. But his job profile and job responsibilities didn't. The president was in no haste. He managed to gather some more information about Albert. He put all the available information together, and discovered some interesting facts.

He later told me that it was quite amazing to find that Albert was a first class graduate. In addition to it, he had a diploma in purchase. But those, whom he was reporting to, were less qualified. Some of them had just managed a degree with a great struggle. It was learnt that Albert was working with this society only because of his family responsibilities.

The president called Albert and had a small session of discussion with him. He found, that as far as the working knowledge was concerned, Albert didn't lack it. He said to

Albert, "Look Mr. Albert, I know it pretty well, and I'm sure, you know it too, that people here are reluctant to work with you. In fact no one wants you in his department. But I still feel the society can make use of your knowledge. In order to make a proper use of your knowledge, we have decided to give you a new assignment from this month onwards. I'm sure, you will prove yourself in this new assignment, and if you do, we will definitely consider you for further elevations."

The next day people saw a new Albert. This new person was willing to cooperate with everyone. No one believed what they saw the next morning. In the coming days Albert changed himself beyond recognition. Those, who avoided talking to him, now wouldn't hesitate to seek his help.

The president told me, he wouldn't have been able to solve the problem, had he not dug up the case a little deeper. A little knowledge of human psychology and natural human behaviour helped him immensely. You sometimes come across such problems, especially when you find that a person is asked to report to someone inferior, or less knowledgeable, or less efficient than himself. No one wants to work under a person, who isn't worth being his boss.

Proper utilisation of talent is a very important function at any workplace. If you have taken over the charge as a unit head, don't ever forget, a lot of your success lies in proper utilisation of manpower. While the correct use of manpower can produce great results, a wrong delegation of powers may cause heavy damage. Imagine about the consequences of elevating a very effective and hard working 'Salesman' to the level of 'Sales Supervisor', overlooking his other assets, just because he has been consistently producing results as a successful salesman. If he displays the qualities of an effective leader, he proves to be an asset. But, if he lacks the leadership qualities, he becomes a liability for the entire set-up. His colleagues, who were coveting a promotion, don't accept him as their boss. They refuse to take orders from him. As a result, the atmosphere of the office is spoiled. The motivation level of all others drops miserably low. If you, as an H.R. Manager promote a wrong guy, and make him a Manager, you suffer a double loss. Want to know how? In the first place, *"you lose a good Salesman"* and in the second place, *"you get a bad Manager"*.

The Human Resources people are, **and they ought to be,** experts of human psychology. This is a very important function, which has a greater tangibility than it shows. It has a direct impact on the results. Therefore, if at any given point of time, you have to play the role of an H.R. Manager, or if you have to select the right person for a promotion from the available lot within your purview, you will find the following points of great use.

I strongly believe that the talent of a human being can be broadly divided into three categories. Or we can also say that there are broadly three types of talents for us to choose from.

1. The first one is like a 'diamond' in a necklace or in a ring you wear on your finger. This type of talent finds the connoisseurs without any effort. This category of talent finds its way in a rather casual manner, and is used more conveniently. It needs no help to glitter, as it has its own glow. Further, the talent falling in this category gets more opportunities than others. So honestly speaking, it doesn't really need a connoisseur to outshine.

2. The second type of talent is also like a 'diamond'. But this diamond harmlessly rests under the layers of dust and rocks, in the depths of a mine, till it is unearthed. And to be dug up, it needs a connoisseur, having the vision of a miner. The glitter of this diamond is no less than the one, falling in the first category, but to use it fruitfully, one needs to recognise its quality, dig it up, and carve it.

If properly used, it returns rich dividends. ***But even if not used, it still remains innocuous for others, and for the whole system.*** People falling in this category are rarely found ambitious. Despite having all the qualities, they rarely nourish ambitions to grow big.

And because they don't nourish ambitions to grow big, they never try to create hurdles for those, who want to grow big and grow fast. They are content with whatever they get, and never approach the bosses, asking for a raise.

But, as a leader you have to be vigilant, and know well, the qualities of such people. If you do, you not only reap large volumes of harvest, but also do justice to such people. And remember, you can't afford to ignore the talent of these people, only because they don't claim. They will never claim. As a leader, you are responsible for their growth. Identify such people. Bring them up. Give them bigger assignments. Make them responsible. Make sure, they grow. Don't fail in recognising these diamonds. Dig them up, carve them, polish them and let them sparkle.

3. The talent falling in this category is the real and biggest challenge. Handling the people falling in this category is a really tough task for those, whom they are reporting to, who have to handle them, take work from them.

The talent falling in this category is like floodwater. And you cannot afford to opt for not using it for any reason. You know how destructive the floodwater can prove if ignored, or left directionless. But every year we see, how engineers use its unlimited energy to irrigate acres of land all over the world. And what do they do to use its unlimited energy in a constructive way?

They construct a dam, and hold it back to form a reservoir. In other words they store its energy, and allow its little streams to run through the canals to irrigate thousands of acres of land. We all know, how destructive it becomes if the same water is allowed to run directionless. Every year we see how hundreds of villages submerge under the floodwater, leaving thousands homeless. Mark it well. **If used in a constructive manner, it gives us life; if not, it becomes a disaster.**

You similarly have some people, who have all the capabilities and necessary knowledge hidden in them, but are always involved in destructive activities, **because they are left free.** Since they have the energy, they can't sit idle.

As a result, they spoil the atmosphere of the office. They create obstructions for others who are willing to work.

The same people prove very useful, if kept busy. They in fact want to be given loads of work. And if entrusted, you find that they are more capable than any other person around them. The problem of such people is that they can't sit idle. They have a tremendous reservoir of energy and willingness to work, this is why they feel embarrassed if their potential is overlooked, or their knowledge is ignored.

You, as a leader must know, such people can't be left free to spoil the atmosphere of the office. They are like flood water. It is up to you, how you use them.

To make the best use of such people, enlist the functions that need more concentration, focused working and a greater level of tenacity. While fixing the job assignment, ensure that they are loaded a little extra. This little extra should be enough to keep them busy. But make sure, they don't feel punished. Make them feel important. Show them and let them feel, you need them. Let them feel, their work is being recognised. Make doubly sure, they take the new assignment as an additional power and enjoy working. Promise them progress, and use their energy for a constructive purpose.

You will find that smartly planned use of available manpower alone will reduce more than half of your workload. And you will find it interesting too. You must know the capabilities and limitations, strengths and weaknesses, of your people. **Remember; they are not always, what they look like.** Some people never talk of their qualities. It is for you, to discover their hidden qualities, and polish them, so that their skill can be used in a proper place.

Remember, you don't have to wander in search of a diamond. Possibly it is there in your pocket. Only you must know it.

I have often seen managers, blaming their subordinates for failures. When caught in a situation, which makes them uncomfortable, they try to save their skin by finding a scape-goat. When in peril, they are shaken, and in such situations they find it easier to put the blame on a person, who is an easy target. In many cases, I have seen managers staying safe by finding a soft target and firing him.

Know it well. Effective leaders never look for solutions in sacking people. Dismissing a person from the job is no solution to any problem. Neither can you expect every person to be Mr. Perfect. Don't ever forget. No one in this world is perfect. Perfection exists only in the imagination.

Such unpleasant situations can be avoided to a great extent if you make sure that the right person handles the right job. And you don't have to look for him. Possibly you already have him in your team. Perhaps your safe is full of 'diamonds'. Be vigilant. Keep your eyes open. Don't fail to identify a diamond. Or else you will be deprived from its natural glow.

□

Remember

You can't blame others for your failures. Neither can you blame your luck. **Luck will favour you only if you prove, you deserve success.**

You have seen how some people rise faster than others around them. Now you know well, which are the qualities that help a person grow. Also you have seen how these qualities have helped people move up the ladder. They weren't born big. Those, you consider successful, have essentially seen failures. It is surely not their luck that has made them, what they are today, but their quality to learn from their mistakes, is what has helped them.

You have seen, how you possess many of the qualities, you feel are necessary for success. Only you didn't know them. Or possibly 'the fire', you already had deep within you, needed to be kindled.

Now that you have seen how these qualities can help you, don't wait. Take the necessary steps to remove the layers of ashes to bring your fire out. And don't be misled. No one will suggest to you, what you should do and what you shouldn't. And why should you need crutches of anybody's help?

Words like bad luck or hard luck are only the creations of the human mind. Luck helps only those, who help themselves. This is the basic truth. The first step has to be taken by you. Only then, will luck take a step to favour you. **But the 'first' step must be initiated by you.** So don't sit waiting for suitable conditions to act upon. They will never be. Waiting for suitable conditions means waiting forever.

Know this universal truth now and remember it. The world of success is uncrowded. Only a few reach the top. Be one of them. Commit to yourself and throw yourself upon the task. You will find that achieving big accomplishments has never been so easy, as you find now. You will find success below your feet. Wish you the best of luck.